T0078320

BEING *Frank* ABOUT VIETNAM

A MARINE PLATOON COMMANDER'S EXPERIENCE

FRANK
HILL

ON THE COVER a photo taken of the author squatting in an 81mm mortar pit at Liberty Bridge, Quang Nam Province, Vietnam, holding a butterfly pin made of finely crafted wire as a gift for his wife. He acquired the jewelry from a Vietnamese vendor in Da Nang for less than $2. The background is a scan of his original combat area map.

Memoir - War - Vietnam

ISBN: 978-1-4817-5715-7 (sc)
ISBN: 978-1-4817-5714-0 (e)

Library of Congress Control Number: 2013909722

Cover and layout design by Stephanie Newton
www.stephill.com
ARNO PRO ITC AVANT GARDE GOTHIC

Printed in U.S.A. | First printing March 2013

10 9 8 7 6 5 4 3 2 1

AuthorHouse™ LLC
1663 Liberty Drive
Bloomington, IN 47403
www.authorhouse.com
Phone: 1-800-839-8640

DEDICATION

To my wife Diana
who weathered the unknown results of war and
has stood by me in the worst of times.

To my daughter Stephanie
who overcame the distance PTSD created
between us and found forgiveness in her heart.

To my son Dusty
whose East African mission work with
Wycliffe Bible Translators confirms my belief
in God that I survived for a purpose.

To all the brave who have served and given
so much to protect our freedom.

No one hates war more than a warrior.
ROBERTA VICTOR

CAPTURED NVA MAP | JANUARY 1969
Circle indicates author's area of operation

ACKNOWLEDGEMENTS

It is with deep gratitude to these dear friends
who brought forth the desire and encouragement to
tell my story. Their support and coaching
will forever be appreciated.

Betty Anne Budy, one of the most caring and encouraging people I know. Our friendship has given Betty a license to challenge me in a positive, loving way to "Keep at it Frank!"

Sheri & Buzz Goff, dear friends from my college days who knew me before the war. Sheri was a social science education major in college. Her feedback was greatly valued. As a fraternity brother, Buzz's encouragement kept the fire burning.

Eileen Law, a friend for the last 40 years who has exceptional editing experience. Eileen's eye for detail exceeded all expectation I had for editing assistance.

Trish Warner McCall, my writing teacher and coach. She volunteers as a writing instructor through Parker United Methodist Church. Trish opened my eyes for the need to give depth and expression to my writing. I hope I have done her justice.

Steve Pierce, a friend of 40 years. His ability to bring clarity and power to words is exceptional. His coaching inspired me to strive for that clarity. I'm forever grateful for his friendship and honest approach to expressing one's self.

Sgt. Ron Powell, my platoon sergeant while fighting in the bush of Vietnam. We fought together, cried together, and bled together. We never end a conversation without saying, "Love you brother!"

Vicki & Bob Russell became lifelong friends during my last year of service at Marine Corps Air Station, Yuma, Arizona. Bob was the station's Naval Supply Officer and tried to keep me on the straight and narrow with vocabulary and spelling when I submitted supply requests, neither of which took root. Vicki currently directs the writing center at Duke University, and her feedback helped greatly in expressing my inner self. I'm indebted to both.

Rev. Gran Smythe, my pastor at Parker United Methodist Church who helped me overcome the guilt of war and accept the forgiveness of our Lord, Jesus Christ.

Jim Winch, with whom I served after returning from Vietnam. His continued support of wounded soldiers on his ranch in Laredo, Texas, continues to inspire me today. I have never known a Marine whose heart was in a better place.

TABLE OF CONTENTS

PREFACE

Carl was ninety years old. Glaucoma had stolen his eyesight. His legs had failed him and his hearing was weak. Yet he greeted me with a brisk, "Hello Frank!" and a hearty handshake when I visited him in his nursing home room. I had known him as my father-in-law for more than forty years, but I would not say our bond was one of a father-son. It was more a bond of mutual respect between kindred spirits. We shared some of the deepest life-impacting experiences a person can have, but at different times. Carl was a World War II veteran who stormed the beaches of Normandy in the second wave of the D-day invasion. I was a Vietnam veteran who experienced the TET Offensive in what was known as the Arizona Territory south of Da Nang. Carl received a Purple Heart for a shrapnel wound in his right hip. My second Purple Heart came from shrapnel in the right thigh just six inches below Carl's wound. We spoke freely of our shared experiences of war, something many veterans are reluctant to do with those who have not felt the pain of a lost comrade or a piece of steel violating their bodies.

As I heard Carl's stories it saddened me to know they would be lost forever as he slipped away in his nursing home bed. I was determined not to let this happen. So I persuaded Carl to let me record our war conversations that focused on his experiences and send the recordings to his children and grandchildren. Doing this made me realize I also needed to tell my story. I owe it to my own children and grandchildren.

But I must admit there are other motivations for telling my story. For example, while at a social event it is common to share your background with others. Upon hearing I served in the Marine Corps, the usual follow-up question is, "Great! Where did you serve?" When I reply "Vietnam," there is a predictable pause as if the other person does not know where to go with the conversation. The moment turns from casual to awkward and usually ends with the other person saying, "Thank you for your service." Or, "You guys really didn't get treated as you should have."

Thanks, but no thanks! I'm not seeking the recognition and honor that was withheld from veterans of Vietnam. I want others to understand what it was like fighting an "endless" war. I want others to know the futility of taking a hill or village only to have the enemy return to occupy it when we left and then having to go back to retake it again and again. It was a war of attrition. Kill as many enemy as you can...Leave and come back to kill more. The pressure from senior command to rack up body count was relentless, and for what purpose?

I'm ready to tell my story. I want to answer questions like, "Are you willing to talk about your experience? What did you do in Vietnam? Where was your unit? Were you ever in a fire fight?" I want an opportunity to separate the political side of war from the human side of war. I want to share what war is like and how it affects those in combat and their families. I want to explain what most men who have sat in the Oval Office have never experienced. Yet, they lead from a position of secure authority, making decisions that impact the lives of thousands serving at their command. It was not until Operation Desert Storm when we kicked Saddam Hussein out of Kuwait that I felt the Vietnam sacrifice had taught our leadership how to conduct a war: get in, get it done, and get out. Unfortunately, these lessons have not taken root.

I recall a quote by Roberta Victor (2003), "No one hates war more than a warrior." It rings true in my heart. I am saddened to see our leaders so quick to start wars when most have never served on the battlefield. Had they, I'm certain their conscience and experience would temper their judgment with the wisdom of knowing the pain that war brings to those serving, as well as to their families. In my opinion, both political parties are guilty of abusing the power of their office by over-reaching with force while not exhausting a course of diplomacy. This ends political commentary in this book. It is time to focus on the human side of war.

Here is my story as straightforward as I can remember it. Many events or brief encounters remain in my memory of the war. Each event is unique in how it developed as well as its final outcome. They are not tied together in a sequence nor are they related. Each event stands on its own as a day-to-day glimpse of real life in the bush of Vietnam. They are snapshots that swim in my memory as a collage of encounters.

Fortunately my wife, Diana, saved every letter I sent her from Vietnam and I've included segments from those letters. I believe these segments reveal in personal detail the stresses of war. Although my prose and spelling in those letters embarrass me today, I hope you understand I was not an English major. I was not concerned about grammatical correctness while under the stress of war. All I wanted to do was get the message across. To improve readability of the letters they have been typed in italics and placed at the end of this book.

For those times when Diana and I were together or when she was impacted through the letters or events at home, she provided her views in her "Reflections" at the end of this book. The page number of her reflection is found following those chapters she referenced in her reflection. Referring to Diana's reflection at the end of those chapters may provide continuity of her perception of the events in that chapter.

In the interest of preserving personal privacy, with the exception of permission by my immediate family and close friends, I have fabricated names to suit the situation. For many encounters I am sad to say I cannot remember most names, but each event and face is indelibly engraved on my memory. Any name used that happens to match that of a Marine who served in Delta Company, 1st Battalion, 5th Marine Regiment from September, 1968 to November, 1969, is coincidental and not reflective of that Marine's performance.

one

PREPARING TO GO

Marine Corps Officer Basic Training was a five-month training course in Quantico, Virginia, located just south of Washington, D.C. The training focused on infantry combat tactics. Every Marine Officer was required to take this course regardless of his future role in the Corps. Even lawyers and pilots took the basic training. It was comforting to know they had an appreciation for infantry terminology and what was required to fight on the ground in Vietnam.

Diana and I arrived in Quantico in April, 1968, having been married less than four months. I had just been commissioned 2nd Lieutenant upon graduation from Colorado State University. I was 22 and Diana was 21. We settled into married officers' quarters, which was a two-story, two-bedroom townhouse. It was a red brick colonial style structure that was built in the mid to late 40's. It was clean and well maintained. We felt fortunate to have nice accommodations after spending the first three months of our marriage in a one-bedroom trailer on a busy street near our college campus. Single officers did not have the luxury of private housing. They lived in dorm-style accommodations near the training complex.

All officers assembled on the parade grounds at 8:00 a.m. each day. It reminded me of boot camp, standing shoulder to shoulder with fellow Marines anxiously anticipating the training

Diana & Mom pinning on my 2nd Lieutenant bars
during the commissioning ceremony.

Our side of the married officer's townhouse.

that was in store for us that day. The major difference was that Captains replaced enlisted Drill Instructors who had harassed us in boot camp. Now that we had been commissioned as officers, it was not appropriate for an enlisted Drill Instructor to degrade us. However, the demeanor of the Captain who now stood in front of us was every bit as demanding as a Drill Instructor. Thankfully, we no longer heard ourselves referred to as "scum bags." Motivating us took on a less personal tone and focused on capability, as in "If you want to stay alive and keep your men alive, listen up!" The reality of being responsible for the lives of others was pounded into us day after day. It was like a mantra I soon became numb to hearing in the training environment. Being responsible for other men's lives was a foregone conclusion. It was part of the drill. It was not until I was in Vietnam that the gut-wrenching reality of making decisions that put the lives of others at risk truly sunk in.

This training was every bit as rigorous as boot camp. We ran the same obstacle courses to keep in shape. The obstacles tested not only our strength and endurance, but also our teamwork. Scaling an eight foot wall and traversing elevated logs required helping my fellow Marines as well as them helping me.

We practiced throwing hand grenades, and then sat in classrooms learning how to call in supporting fire from artillery and fighter jets. The Basic School even had a mock Vietnamese Village for teaching us how to approach and enter a "vill."

Finally the day came when we had to declare our Military Occupation Specialty (MOS). Many had already designated their MOS upon Corps entry, but some of us had yet to declare. My options were armor, supply, or infantry. I did not struggle with the decision. It was infantry for me. Having observed the challenges of command, I wanted to lead. However, I must be honest and say that after making my choice I took a deep breath and asked myself, "What have you gotten yourself into?"

Basic Training concluded with graduation in August. In

The obstacle course with Diana leaning
on one of the scaling walls.

Training village at Quantico, VA.

commemoration the school put on an event called "Mad Moment." This was a display of fire power using artillery, mortars and machine guns. It was similar to the grand finale of a fireworks show. However, I question the comfort it gave our wives knowing their husbands would soon experience their own "mad moments."

Following graduation everyone got their orders for their next duty stations. Without surprise, my orders directed me to report to the 1st Marine Division in Da Nang, Vietnam. Diana and I had one month to move our belongings back to Colorado, visit our friends and relatives, and make plans to go to my departure point, Travis Air Force Base, Sacramento, California.

My sister, her husband, and their three children had moved to Sacramento, as had my father upon his retirement. I was fortunate to have close family see me off at my departure point. Diana and I flew to Sacramento to spend our last week together with family.

After arriving in California, we took a few days to relax by ourselves in Lake Tahoe. It was there, in a casino near the lake, that we had our first disagreement of any consequence. I think the stress of my leaving for war had each of us worried about future events. The last day, as we walked through the casino on our way out of the resort, I took a twenty-dollar bill and pitched it on the roulette table. I did not care where it landed and don't remember the number where the bill rested. I was tempting fate and wanted some indication of my luck. The dealer spun the wheel and I watched the ball spin and fall to a number that was not where my $20 was resting. The dealer scooped up the money. We continued on our journey back to Sacramento.

Diana was clearly upset. Her smile changed to an expressionless stare as if she questioned my sanity. I had just thrown $20 away as casually as if I had flushed it down the toilet. Later she shared her feelings and concern for my careless action. $20 was a lot of money in 1968 and she would be on her own once I departed. It was as if I did not care for her well-being and had resigned myself to the tragedy of war. As for me, I agreed it was a selfish act, but I had no concern for the value of money. I would be on a plane the next day headed for a war that concerned me far greater than $20. The uncertainty of not knowing if I would return was ever-present and made it difficult to enjoy the last few hours I had with Diana. However, to her credit, she did not dwell on my casual gambling misfortune and maintained a strong, positive attitude right up to kissing me good-bye when she boarded the plane back to Denver.

After seeing Diana off, my dad drove me to Travis Air Base. I expected to board a military transport, but to my surprise it was an American Airlines 707. Our destination was Camp Hansen in Okinawa. The flight was crammed full of Marines, none of whom I knew from training in Quantico. Everyone was absorbed in his own thoughts. Some read. Some slept. Few engaged in conversation. Laughter was nonexistent. It was like when you are scared as hell and don't want to show it. After fourteen hours the plane landed in Okinawa and we boarded buses for transport to Camp Hansen.

My stay at Camp Hansen was short-lived, only two days, since this was just a layover point for the final four-hour flight to Da Nang. I attended some final briefings on illness prevention, personal hygiene, malaria medication, and received a bunch of inoculations for every possible disease known to man.

Cheap pawn shops ringed the entrance gate to the camp. I took advantage of the short layover to load up on some things I felt I might need in Vietnam: waterproof wrist watch and a rain suit. Someone had left behind a pair of jungle boots in my room. They appeared to be much better suited for the jungle than the all-leather combat boots I was wearing. The discarded boots had a canvas upper that allowed for better breathing and evaporation. I tried them on and they fit, so I kept them for the final leg of my journey.

Diana C. Hill
900 Applewood Ave.
Littleton, Colo. 80120

VIA AIR MAIL

The monsoons are here and it
will be pretty wet for the next
6 months. We got some shots
to-day, one was in the butt and
it sure did hurt. Malaria pills
and what not. This is a cool
base wish my tour was here.
We had a secret briefing to day
and it scared the poop right out
of me. I went to cash sales and
picked up a few sock, skivies,
I set Utilities and found some
old boots someone threw away.
They will at least get me
to Nam and save poo

They have Mama Sans here
that Comin, clean your room wash
clothes shine shoes for 75¢ a
Taxi any where is 25¢ drinks
in the Officers bare are 30¢ I
wonder what happy hour is like.
Well I need to get a hair cut (35¢)
and it is next to the Post offices
plus. I'm going to the Gift shop.
Now, if they will mail it you can
expect something but if they don't
I can't take time to, we have to leave
for the plane by 2000 hr, I'll
be getting my plt. To morrow I guess.
It is like a foot-ball game I'm scard
to death but hope to settle down when
The ACTION starts. I know you are sleeping
now or you should be, pleasent dreams
I miss you very much because there
was one hell of an emptyness when you
got on that plan I will I would have
kissed you more
                    your loving Husband
                    all ways Frank.

two

ARRIVAL IN VIETNAM

We boarded a commercial jet for the final flight to Da Nang. I was surprised to see women as the attendants on our flight into a combat zone. I expected to see military personnel working on the plane, but it was regular airline employees.

The four-hour flight from Okinawa to Da Nang seemed short. The reality of landing in a war zone filled me with gut-wrenching fear. Circles of sweat in my arm pits showed a clear sign of fear, not exercise.

As we landed I expected to hear the distant activity of war, that sound of explosions in the distance as if the fighting was just a few miles away. It was surprisingly quiet. Had I not known we had landed in a war zone, I would have thought we had returned to Okinawa. Having watched war movies as a youth, I had an unrealistic expectation of the sound of war. Soon I would discover fighting was brief, intense, and unexpected. Bullets did not whistle past. Instead, they made a snapping sound like someone clapping their hands next to your ear like miniature sonic booms.

We disembarked down a gangway. No sooner than the last man's boots hit the ground did the door close on the plane, the gangway pulled away, and the plane taxied to the main runway and departed. Now I understood why a commercial jet could be used to bring us to Da Nang. It could not have been on the ground more than twenty minutes and the landing strip was very well secured.

We boarded a bus that delivered us to Division Headquarters for check-in and unit assignment. Upon checking in I learned I would be assigned to Delta Company, 1st Battalion, 5th Marines. Little did I know this was a highly decorated unit that served in Hue during the TET Offensive just a few months earlier. I was told Delta Company was awarded the Presidential Unit Citation, which is exceptional for a unit the size of a company (approximately 200 men). I was really starting to worry. I was getting assigned to a real kick-butt unit and I knew who would get the toughest assignments when the shit hit the fan.

An Hoa was the base for the 5th Marines. It was about twenty miles south of Da Nang. Getting there proved problematic since the monsoons had descended, causing flightsto be restricted and making the roads nearly impassable.

Oct. 19
0700

Diana!

We are still in Division rear trying to get to Anihoa where the 5th regiment is located. Just sitting here for 3 days gives me little to write about; So I'm going to give you a mental picture of division rear. The buildings are all on stilts about 1 or 2 ft. high constructed of ply wood and tin roof, screens are most of the walls. We have one cot and blanket to sleep on and this is more than most of the troops have. They sleep in their poncho on the floor. "No hot water and there are water hours. Trucks are running all over the place, we are near the 11ᵗʰ Motor transport area. The urinal is a 55 gal. drume in the ground and the Crsper is just an out door head. The perimiter is about ½ mile on ¾ of this hill and last nite I was going to the head and noticed a few tracers zipping off the hill and a few hand grenades going off.

OCTOBER 19, 1968 | DA NANG | TYPESET PAGE 220

Oct 21
1810

Dear Diana,

It is 7:10 where you are and I'm finally in An Hoa with mud ankle deep. We finally got on a helo and in 15 min. here we are. Boy! this has to be a first writting you too letters in the same day with in 8 hours. But enjoy it while you can you may not get but one a week or less while I'm in the field. So don't worry if you don't get a letter right off the bat! ok? Every day that is. There was nothing but water between Da Nang & An Hoa!

Now I can see why it is so difficult to get in here. I wish they would give me a weapon I would feel a little better. We have been didy-bopping around where anybody could come in and hit us. I think I'll write more when I get to my battalion.

The platoon commander that preceded me was killed by an ambush, Aug. 29th So know my rattle is really shaken up. Delta 1/5 is the best in the Bn they have killed the most NVA & VC and like-wise taken more casualties. I'm worried but It must be worth it or I would not be here. Would I? Arty (Artillery) is really pounding away tonight I wonder if I'll get any sleep to nite. Don't forget my absent T Ballot although I believe it is too late now! The Time is now or never. Let it be now! OH God, I pray I want to see you again!

Good night
Love Frank.

Okay, reality was setting in and I was so scared I couldn't eat or sleep. I was taking in the sights, sounds and smell of war. The night sky was illuminated with flares hanging from small parachutes as they drifted slowly to the ground. They made the perimeter of the camp clearly visible so men in their bunkers could see any enemy who might try to sneak close enough to throw a grenade. Every two or three hours the blasts of 105mm Howitzers shook me from a deep sleep. When I realized it was us shooting, my exhaustion took over and I quickly fell back to sleep.

I was starting to feel the pressure of having to put on a facade of self-confidence so I wouldn't lose the respect of my men when I took command of my platoon. The anxiety of sitting on the sidelines and watching the war unfold was like walking through a door and not knowing what awaits you on the other side, knowing the reality will not be pleasant. My weight was declining rapidly; this resulted in diminished stamina. I felt weak all the time, and my lack of resistance made the slightest scratch fester into an oozing, pus-filled boil. The men referred to these infections as "gook sores."

Oct 23
21:00

Diana,

It is 10:00 am, Oct. 23 in Colo. now. I'll bet there is a frost in the air and the back range is pure white. This country could be beautiful if their was no war going on. I'm going to the bush Sat. the 26th. I don't know if you got that paper I sent or not, but I'm taking over the 1st Plt., the one that

13

Supper in the Horseshoe after joining my platoon.
Notice the tall elephant grass and the
Song Thu Bon River in the distance.

The Horseshoe – taken from the helicopter that
delivered me to my platoon.

was over ran. With hand to hand combat. But don't worry that very rarely happens. A fantom jet made an air strick just outside of the perimeter this morning. It looks like a little bug then bright lights jet out from under its wings (Rockets) and it pulls up and through the Clouds. Now they are firing those illumination rounds into the "Arizona" area north of us. (Refer to Paper "Sea Tiger") I'll be joining the Co. when they are in that region. If this type of stuff bugs you let me Know & I won't write it.

OCTOBER 23, 1968 | AN HOA | TYPESET PAGE 222

On November 4, 1968, I finally reached my platoon in the bush. Instead of operating with the other platoons in Delta Company, my platoon was temporarily assigned to Charlie Company in a notorious area called the "Horseshoe," a large bend in the river that resembled an upside-down horseshoe on the map. I hooked a ride to my new platoon on a resupply chopper that afternoon.

As I got off the chopper I was greeted by the acting platoon commander, Staff Sergeant Richards, and his backup, Sergeant Powell. Both men smiled and greeted me warmly as if I were a long-lost friend. They seemed happy to have an officer to collaborate with and share responsibility.

Assuming command of a combat unit deployed in the bush is tricky business. One wrong step out of the gate can cost you the respect and confidence of your men. Being a dictator and "know-it-all" was not my style, nor something I was prepared to do. Since I did not know any of the men or their capabilities, I had to rely heavily on both Richards and Powell. I had rehearsed and role-played this meeting in my mind many times. I desperately wanted to get off on the right foot.

After dropping my pack and making small talk about our backgrounds, I pulled Richards and Powell aside so we could have a private conversation. I made it clear to both men I respected their time in the bush and planned to rely heavily on their experience and knowledge of the men's capabilities. I wanted their input and suggestions on every key decision and how to stay alive in the bush.[1] I would make the final determination, but made sure they knew their input was critical. I could see from their faces that a mutual relationship of respect was starting to take shape.

1. In the course of writing this memoir I had the great fortune of reconnecting with Sgt. Ron Powell. He returned to Massachusetts after recuperating from his war wounds and makes his home there today. There is a special love between men who fight in battles and rely on each other to stay alive. It is an unshakable brotherly bond that transcends time. While reminiscing about when we first met, Sgt. Ron graced me with the following quote from an email he sent in February 2012:

> *Frank,*
>
> *I'm still just as proud of you now as I was when we served to-gether. I still remember the day we met in AN Hoa. You introduced yourself and the first thing you asked was. " What do I have to do to stay alive" I knew then that you would be a man I would die for when the time came. I'm glad it didn't come to that but we came close a few times.*
>
> *I have never reminisced about the war without including your name and your courage in those stories. Our bond will always be ironclad Lt. Frank and beyond reproach.*
>
> *I love you buddy, Sgt. Ron*

three

CHARLIE COMPANY

Operating with a company other than Delta, my assigned company, did not excite me. I was looking forward to meeting the Delta company commander and start building relationships with my fellow platoon commanders. I was not told how long my platoon would be assigned to Charlie Company and that gave me a sense of detachment like an orphan in an unfamiliar family.

Charlie Company was conducting a blocking operation. Most blocking operations are aimed at preventing enemy troops from moving to an objective, or engaging them while they retreated from the pressure of other units advancing on them.

The blocking operation was being conducted at the top of the Horseshoe inside the loop that was formed by the Song Thu Bon River. The land mass within the Horseshoe was three to four square miles, considerably more territory than one company could effectively conduct operations. Therefore, our temporary attachment to Charlie Company was to help prevent enemy movement out of the Horseshoe and across the river, as well as to supplement their search and destroy activities.

Search and destroy is exactly that. We searched for the enemy in bunkers, villages, and the bush (rice paddies and jungle). We searched for caches of weapons and food. When we found the enemy it was usually because they fired on us first.

Captured AK-47 assault rifle.

Food and clothing cache found buried in a bunker

Occasionally we would find an unarmed young man of fighting age and validate his credentials, which had been issued to Vietnamese citizens by the Government of South Vietnam. Failure to provide these credentials resulted in being taken into custody and shipped out on the next resupply chopper for interrogation at regimental headquarters. If someone was running when challenged to stop, or was carrying a weapon, it was a license to be fired upon. Most encounters where we took enemy fire occurred at dusk or during the night. The enemy was bold under the cover of darkness. They would sneak as close as possible to our position, throw hand grenades, or fire a quick burst from their automatic weapons and run. This tactic required them to hide their weapons during the day.

Searching for caches of weapons and food was difficult. The Viet Cong (VC) had ingenious methods when it came to hiding weapons. On one occasion while crossing a waist-deep stream, one of the men behind me tripped over something. When he reached down in the water to pull up what had tripped him, he discovered an AK-47 assault rifle wrapped in plastic.

I was not excited about my platoon being loaned out to Charlie Company. Once I met the company commander, Captain Sanderson, my worst fears became suddenly realized. He was tall, about six feet three inches, and thin as a rail. He walked with a slight hunch that made him appear to be looking down at the ground and down at me in a condescending manner even though I was only two inches shorter. He had been called up from the Marine Reserves into active duty. As a result his attitude was as sour as rotten grapes and I could see he and I would not be hitting it off. He did not ask some getting-to-know-you questions like: "How long have you been in the bush?" "How are your men doing?" "Need anything?" Instead he plopped down a map showing the Horseshoe and pointed to a location along the river that ran about 900 meters and said, "Get your men up there and set in along the river!" I immediately realized the risk involved and replied, "Captain, that is a huge area to cover with only 32 men and we will not be able to protect our rear." Sanderson was clearly agitated by my concern. He raised his head, looked me in the eye with a squint and replied, "Get it done, Lieutenant!" Without saying another word, I picked up my rifle and walked away to join my men. We headed for the top of the Horseshoe. This asshole was clearly not concerned about a platoon that was temporarily assigned to him. He was going to look out for his own men at our expense.

Nov. 10.

Dearest Diana,

We left for the field 3 days ago. I've had 2 men wounded by friendly fire. I'll try to tell as much as I can so it will be messy. My platoon is by our selves working with another Co. up in the Horse Shoe. I set up a tight perimiter the night of the 7th in a small vill about 25 meters by 50 meters. The tree line came right up to our perimiter about 5:00 the next morning we got a few hand grenades from VC thrown our way they landed just at the edge of our perim. Scared the shit right out of me. I don't think I've slept 2 hr since. Earlier that day my point men came up on a VC running across a sandy area into the tall grass, I called in 18 81mm mortar rounds but did not get him. he

was out of, small arms range. So
far I haven't had a rifle round in
my direction but a hand grenade is
bad enough. From that hill we moved

North into the "horse shoe" to
link up with Charlie Company.
they have the NVA backed up against
the river and they need my plt. to
fill a gap in the lines. Ever since
we have been here we have been getting
screwed. We have gotten only 1 mean
a day and doing most of the work. We
have a larger perimeter than the other
platoons and they have no discipline.
Last night my machine gun team captured
two men of military age hiking out. I
believe them to be VC or NVA. However
the company commander is disagreeing
with me. he is a Capt. & me a Lt. what
the hell can it do. well I'll tell you
this is not like basic school
I'm bitchin and he doesn't like it a
bit to God damn bad. I'm here to
look out for my men. And I don't
call putting 32 men over a 900
meter line looking after them.

It was late one evening and the sun was fading quickly when one of the machine gun teams on our right flank detected movement. The Marines fired a warning burst and challenged the two figures moving in the dim light. They raised their arms high over their heads and quickly gave themselves up. Their clothing was white, which would have made them easily detectable during the night, so it was doubtful they had planned to sneak up and harass us with grenades or small arms fire. They appeared to be fighting age, mid to late twenties, but had no identification that showed them to be South Vietnamese.

My Command Post (CP) was situated in the middle of the 900 meter line that we had established on the bank of the river, so I was shocked when one of my machine gun teams entered the CP after dark with two prisoners blindfolded. It was a long walk for them after dark. One of the Vietnamese had a bruised and swollen cheek. When I asked what happened the response was, "He resisted the blindfold, so we had to convince him it was necessary." I was satisfied with their response. It was important to blindfold any detainee. Otherwise, if they were truly VC or North Vietnamese Army (NVA), and happened to escape, they would be able to report our location and troop strength.

Since they were the first Vietnamese we had taken into custody, I couldn't be sure they were not the enemy. They certainly looked like non-combatants, but I was not willing to take any chances since they did not have proper identification. Also, it was not uncommon for VC or NVA to surrender in the hopes of becoming a Kit Carson Scout.[1]

It was dark. We bound their arms and feet and kept them in the CP overnight. They slept on the ground between two men to make sure they did not escape. Upon daylight I allowed pictures to be taken before we delivered the prisoners to Captain Sanderson's CP.

When I arrived at Sanderson's CP he questioned me as to the treatment of the detainees when he saw one had been

The two men we took into custody while in the Horseshoe.
I'll never know if these men had been VC or NVA.
If not, I'm glad their lives were spared.

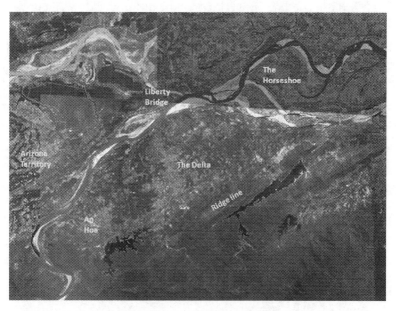

Area of operation for 1st Battalion, 5th Marine Regiment,
1st Marine Division; located 20 miles south of Da Nang.
Delta Company worked mainly in the Horseshoe, Delta and Liberty
Bridge areas with occasional sorties in the Arizona Territory.

roughed up. I explained what my men had reported to me. He read me the riot act for mistreatment of prisoners and informed me that he felt those men could not be VC or NVA soldiers. When I explained they did not have the proper identification, he brushed me off and said, "We'll send them in for interrogation and see about that." I never got confirmation if they were NVA, VC or civilians.

After two more days we finished our operation in the Horseshoe and returned to Battalion Headquarters at Liberty Bridge for five days of recuperation. I was so pissed with Sanderson that I asked for a meeting with the Battalion Executive Officer, Lieutenant Colonel Johnson. When I met with Johnson I told him Sanderson was not fit to command. I explained the reckless order to cover 900 meters of river with only 32 men and Sanderson's rebuff when I turned over detainees to him. Then I made the fatal mistake one should never do in a combat situation. I told Johnson, "There is no way I'm going back to the bush with Sanderson!" Johnson's reply was simple and direct, "Lieutenant, failure to comply with an order will result in immediate court-martial!" That certainly got my attention. So I tucked my tail between my legs and retreated to join my men at the Bridge. My platoon would be assigned back to my original company, Delta Company, and start operations under Captain Gilson. To this day I wonder if my complaint about Sanderson had any impact on the decision for my platoon rejoining Delta Company.

1. The term "Kit Carson Scout" was developed from our western history of recruiting scouts from opposing Indian tribes to help guide and interpret encounters with hostile tribes. They knew the lingo of the enemy and spoke broken English. They knew what questions to ask and how to interrogate captives.

four

THE WATER BUFFALO

We had just finished a week of duty at Liberty Bridge (Battalion Headquarters). Platoons would be rotated out of the bush every 8 to 10 weeks to help guard the perimeter of Liberty Bridge, and everyone looked forward to our "vacation" at the "Bridge": two hot meals daily, a chance to wash off, and naps during the day—aaaah, heaven!

Our orders directed us to occupy an area about four miles southeast of the bridge. The mission was the standard routine for working this area: search for weapon caches and look for opportunities to engage the Viet Cong. This was a fertile rice paddy area with scattered vills about a half mile from each other.

The first village we approached was about a mile east of the main road that ran south from Liberty Bridge to An Hoa. There was no direct route to the village from the road, so we had to travel through tree lines that wound around rice paddies. What should have been a 20-minute hike turned into an hour. The village rested on an egg-shaped knoll that rose four to five feet above the rice paddies that surrounded it. Eight to ten hooches (the slang term we used for a thatched-roof hut or a simple dwelling) occupied the knoll in a cluster no more than ten paces apart. It appeared to be a village for an extended family - grandparents, children and grandchildren.

It was late afternoon, clear skies and warm... maybe mid 80's. We all had our green camouflage towels looped over the back of our necks to wipe the sweat from our faces. The sun turned our helmets into solar furnaces. Most men had nothing on under their flak vest. However, I preferred a T-shirt under my flak vest to help buffer my side from the rubbing of the shoulder holster that held my standard issue 45-caliber pistol.

The plan was to move through the village and set up for the night a few hundred yards past the village. We avoided setting up defensive positions in vills. Finding concealed positions for protection and clear fields of fire was difficult among the structures. Communication was also hampered with the hustle and bustle of the villagers, and setting up inside the village put them in harm's way.

As we approached the village there was much activity visible. Kids played and women worked among the hooches. Lots of activity was always a good sign as it indicated a low probability that "unfriendlies" could be in the village and open fire on us. Once we entered and passed by the first hooch, the mama-sans gathered their kids together and avoided eye contact with us. They took on a humble posture with hunched shoulders, while looking down at the ground and appearing to go about their business. Some appeared to make busy work by suddenly sweeping the loosely woven mats on the dirt floor of their hooch.

As I rounded the corner of a hooch I came face to face with a Vietnamese woman leading a large water buffalo and a calf. Water buffaloes are the tractors of the Vietnamese. Although having been in the bush for only a few months I had never come face to face with a water buffalo; however, I had heard stories of their ill temperament. They are black with sweeping horns that curl up at the tips with a span of three to four feet from tip to tip. Their dark, penetrating eyes make them an imposing sight. Their shoulders and haunches are built for power. A mature water buffalo is the size of a rodeo Brahma bull standing five to six feet tall at the shoulders. They work in the rice paddies pulling logs behind them to level the floor of the paddy. A level surface allows the water to have an even depth for growing rice. They are accustomed to the Vietnamese and quite docile and compliant with their commands. Even young children can ride and lead them. Not so with strangers and especially Marines. I'm sure our helmets and bulky flak vests made us look like creatures from another world, and water buffaloes would become quickly agitated and unpredictable at the sight of us.

The Vietnamese motivate and guide their buffalo with frequent swats on the rump from a long stick. Most Vietnamese "park" their water buffaloes next to their hooch. The buffalo is placed in a pit about three feet deep with mud up to the buffalo's belly. The back of the pit has just enough incline to lead the animal into it. A nose ring with a rope is often used to tether the animal and a simple pole fence about three-feet high surrounds the edge. This fence is not meant to keep the buffalo in the pit, but rather to keep children from falling into a three foot hole. The pit alone is designed to keep the buffalo confined. An animal the size of a horse in a three-foot hole with mud up to its belly would have a very difficult time escaping.

The buffalo was so close that I could have reached out and touched her nose. I jumped back as she gave a loud snort. The calf bolted and tried to escape from our encounter. The buffalo was defending its calf and directed all her attention on me. I started to retreat backward as the Vietnamese woman pulled on the rope attached to the buffalo's nose ring. There was no way a 100-pound woman could restrain a 2000-pound buffalo intent on ripping me to shreds. The buffalo was so focused on me I felt like a rabbit being pursued by a wolf. All I wanted to do was get away. I continued to back up, grasping for the safety on my rifle. I could hear the Marines behind me flipping their safeties on their M-16s to fire. I began yelling, "Don't shoot, don't shoot!" I still hoped the woman could restrain the buffalo, but the woman was being dragged while her heels dug into the ground. The struggle was intense. The buffalo had no other objective, but to get the guy who threatened her and her calf. The struggle continued. I was still retreating and fumbling to find my safety. What seemed like minutes was actually less than five seconds. Finally, my safety clicked off and I squeezed the trigger. I'm sure most of my shots hit the ground as I was stumbling backwards. I remember yelling "Shoot!" I don't know if it was my command to fire or my shots that signaled two Marines to open fire, but thankfully they did. The buffalo fell to the ground, dead, just a few feet from me. Relief filled me and I tried to collect myself. I was at a loss for words. While thankful for the action of my men to protect me, I was upset we had to kill the mother of a calf. The three or four villagers standing nearby said nothing, but I could sense their sadness and contempt. All I could do was tell my point man to move on through the village.

As we moved on to our objective for the night, I reflected on the indoctrination given to all officers entering Vietnam. The message was to win hearts. Wow, how many hearts did I win today? We had just eliminated a major source of survival for those hearts we were supposed to win. That night I radioed Battalion Headquarters and explained the situation. They said the next platoon moving through that village would have a public relations officer and would compensate their loss. I have no idea if that ever happened.

Nov. 19.

Dearest Diana

We have been moving all over,
Mostly collecting rice and flying it
out. Yesterday my platoon found
3500 lbs of rice in 3 pouches (homes)
we sacked it and called in a helo,
as the chopper was lifting it out
we started to take sniper fire
we returned fire and the chopper
made it out. Then we got
the hell out of there and bombed
the shit out of them. We charged
our possition and last night one
of our patrols was hit by gooks.
No casualties, but on the way in
this morning they triped a Booby
trap and one person recieved
minor wounds. "Lucky" But
here is the kicker. Today I
made my first kill and all most
got it in the processes. I took
my plt. out this morning on
patrol, as we intered this vill
to check for I D's and VC
suspects, this mans son came
around the corner of a Houch

Loading a water Buffalo and a calf. Man that was all she wrote the Buffalo started to charge me I kicked my M-16 of Safty and retreated doing a nifty back step while at the same time pumping rounds in to the huge beast baring down on me. Then I stumbled and Brayton (a trooper on my right opend up.) The force of his bullets striking the buffalo knocked it off balance and it missed me by a few feet. He finally dropped dead about 10 ft. away. Needless to say I was shook up, that is the closest call I've had here. yet. But I'm sure there will be closer and not with water buffalos.

TYPED LETTER FORMAT IS LOCATED ON PAGE 223

five

KID DIGGIN' A HOLE

We had finished sweeping through an area north of An Hoa and south of Liberty Bridge. It was time to find a suitable place to set up for the night. The goal was to find a high point and ring the top of the hill with our foxholes and fire teams. We found just such a hill overlooking the main supply road to An Hoa. It had a commanding view of the road and the valley below.

Each position on the perimeter had three men. Three men together allowed a rotation of 2 hours awake, 4 hours of sleep. Some would dig a foxhole, but it was not like the foxholes we had seen in the movies where a soldier could sit or stand in the hole waist deep. No, we just carved out depressions about a foot deep so we could lie prone and hope shrapnel from a mortar or a bullet would skip over us.

As the sun was starting to fall in the west, we dropped our packs and began to inflate our rubber ladies (aka air mattresses). Some of the men had already broken open their C-rations and started to heat them with C-4. C-4 is a very stable plastic explosive. It comes in blocks about 10 inches long, 1 inch thick and 2 inches wide. One block weighs about a pound. Its consistency is like putty and it reminded me of a Big Hunk candy bar. A bullet could penetrate it and it would not explode, but a blasting cap provided enough force to explode it. Once it exploded it was intensely powerful. Half a block of C-4 could sever a steel beam on a bridge. However, using C-4 to heat C-rations was fairly safe. This was not something we learned in basic training. I was introduced to cooking with C-4 soon after taking command of my platoon. We would pull off a piece and roll it in the palm of our hands to form a ball the size of a golf ball. Once we had the ball formed we pinched the side of the ball to form a protrusion the size of a finger nail. This protrusion was the ignition point. Now, all we had to do was light the protrusion and the rest of the ball would become inflamed with an intense heat. One C-4 ball could bring a canteen cup of water to a boil in two minutes. Using the blue heating tabs from the C-ration kits was a waste of time because their flame was slow and weak. It took three to four times longer to heat a meal with the heating tabs.

I folded my half-inflated rubber lady to form a comfortable sitting stool and pulled out my maps. It was time to set up our on-call fire for the night. Setting up on-call fire is routine every night. Basic School infantry training placed a great deal of emphasis on how to set up on-call fires. I radioed the Battalion Fire Control Center at Liberty Bridge and gave them our position. The 105 howitzers at Liberty Bridge were only about 4 miles north of us, so we were well within their range. Then I selected three to four fire points (coordinates: exact locations using north/south east/west degrees/minutes/seconds) around our position where artillery fire could be activated with one quick call should we get attacked at night. The key to setting up an on-call fire is to select the most vulnerable approaches to our position. A trench or depression leading to our lines or thick jungle next to us made the best candidates for setting up points of on-call fire. There would be no time to figure out where you want the artillery when you're getting attacked at night. It is much easier to just call the fire control center and say, "We need fire on alpha one." The last resort on-call fire point was our position, should the enemy overrun our lines.

After I had established our on-call fires with the Battalion Fire Control Center, I got my C-ration out of my pack to prepare supper. As I stood on top of the hill with the C-rations in my hand I noticed a young boy riding a water buffalo on the road below us. I guessed his age to be thirteen or fourteen. He was heading in our direction and appeared to be returning home from working in the rice paddies. He stopped his water buffalo just below our position, dismounted and knelt next to the side of the road. It was certain he did not know a platoon of Marines was on the hill overlooking him about 600 yards away.

I was curious as to his motives and called over Sergeant Powell. "That kid just got off his water buffalo and is on his knees on the side of the road."

Sgt. Powell looked through his binoculars. "Looks like he is digging a hole."

"Do you think he is setting a booby trap?" I asked.

"I don't know, Lieutenant, but there is no reason for him to be digging there."

"Tell the snipers to get over here right now!" I commanded in an angry tone. I was pissed that this kid was doing something suspicious that might kill Marines. I had to take some action against him. The main supply route to An Hoa was notorious for booby traps disabling convoys. I was not willing to take any chances that this kid was setting a trap.

Within a minute the sniper team joined me and Sergeant Powell with their sniper rifle and the spotting scope used by the spotter. Most platoons are assigned a sniper team of two Marines. One is the spotter and one is the shooter. Our sniper team was Corporal Ramsey and Lance Corporal Grimes. Both men proved themselves to be outstanding marksmen. They had already recorded a confirmed kill at 1100 meters (3/4 mile). I had great confidence in their accuracy.

Sniper teams are some of the bravest Marines I have ever encountered. At times they are fearless beyond reason. They would eat an early supper and go outside the defense perimeter just before dark. They would find a good observation point where they could use their night vision scopes and spend the entire night looking for targets. Occasionally we would hear a single shot and knew they had done their job.

Corporal Ramsey was the shooter. His weapon was a Remington Model 700 bolt action rifle (M40), noted for its long distance accuracy. It was chambered for the 7.62mm NATO bullet. Both the bullet weight and powder charge had been specially matched for optimum distance and accuracy. Lance Corporal Grimes was the spotter. The spotter was vital to the success of the sniper team. He was able to calculate the distance to the target within a few feet. But, more importantly, he was able to tell the shooter cross wind speed between them and the target. Cross winds of a few miles per hour can greatly affect the accuracy of a bullet at long distances.

I explained the situation to Ramsey and Grimes. They got into position with Ramsey on his belly in the prone shooting position. The stock of the rifle was in his shoulder and the bipod on the front of the barrel was extended and resting on the ground to steady the rifle. Grimes crossed his legs in a sitting position with his spotting scope on a tripod between his legs. Grimes was crisp and methodical, "Range 530 meters, no wind, clear to the target." Ramsey made the appropriate adjustments to his rifle scope, pulled back the bolt to insert the bullet and asked, "Lieutenant, where do you want the round...on the kid or the buffalo?"

I looked through my binoculars and could see the kid still digging. The buffalo was standing broadside to us and appeared very docile. The kid was on the other side of the buffalo just under the buffalo's neck. I replied, "Neither; put the round in the dirt right under the buffalo's nose." All I wanted to do was send a message...get the hell out of here...you have no business digging on the side of the road.

Ramsey replied, "Yes, sir." He closed the bolt on the rifle, paused for 10-15 seconds... BOOM! The round was on its way. A cloud of red dust flew up into the buffalo's nostrils. The buffalo spun around and galloped down the road from where they had come. The kid was up and running with all his might following the buffalo. From what we could see the kid never caught up to the buffalo as they rounded a far bend and out of sight. We chuckled, patted each other on the back, and went back to our C-rations. We had sent a message without taking a life. I slept well that night.

six

FRIENDLY VILLS

Village life was difficult and I felt sorry for how these people had to cope with two warring factions, us by day and the VC by night. Some vills greeted us in a friendly manner while others seemed withdrawn and preferred to see us leave as soon as possible. I recall two friendly villages that welcomed us and showed hospitality by sharing what little they had.

During patrols we encountered only women, children and old men as occupants in the villages. It was difficult to understand how these simple people could exist on this land without the help of young men. The women and children, up to the age of twelve, worked in the rice paddies from sunup to sundown. Then they would return from the field and prepare dinner over an open fire. They had simple meals, mostly boiled rice with a few vegetables mixed in, a little onion, maybe some tender bamboo shoots. On a special occasion a bit of chicken might be added. I remember one village where a mama san offered me a bowl of food from her dinner pot. Maybe it was the repetitive, mundane taste of C-rations, or the welcoming gesture of sharing a meal with her family, but whatever it was, the moment caught me off guard and I felt a need to accept the gesture of hospitality. I did not expect to like the small bowl of rice handed to me. However, I found the contents to be a flavorful treat. The amount of rice was meager, a cup at most. It had a spicy snap, which I liked. I wolfed it down with great gusto, putting the edge of the bowl to my lower lip and scooping the rice in my mouth with the chop sticks just like mama san and papa san. After rinsing out the bowls, they retired to their beds on a thatched mat in the corner of their hooch. I joined my men just a few yards outside the vill.

I hated the grime and filth of being in the bush. Three to four weeks without a bath or shower drove us to take knife baths. Yes, a knife bath actually worked. While the sweat was still rolling off our bodies we could take a knife and scrape it across our arms, legs and torso, taking off a layer of dirt, grime and loose skin. The residue on the knife blade looked like gray mud. Although not getting us truly "clean," it at least gave our pores some air to breathe and I could again feel the coolness of the air on my body. Unfortunately, this did nothing for the odor that permeated all of us, but there was no one to offend and we all became accustomed to the stink of ourselves.

If we had the good fortune to be near a river, we would jump in with all our clothes on and scrub with a bar of soap over our clothes as if washing ourselves in a shower. This got some of the grime out of our clothing. Then we would strip down and wash our bodies. Once finished we would retrieve our "washed" clothes and put them on wet. Wearing wet clothes did not bother us. Having wet clothes from washing was far better than wet clothes from sweat!

We had set in on a low hill overlooking a small vill next to a large rice paddy. The vill had only three or four hooches. We had not washed in the river for a long time and had become very grungy. Sgt. Powell and I decided to go to the vill at the bottom of the hill and see if we could find some water to get the grime off of us. As we entered the vill an elderly white-haired man greeted us. He seemed happy to see us and most welcoming. He put his hands together under his chin and bowed to greet us. It was like he was welcoming royalty to his village. The Vietnamese knew how to play the game of survival. During the day we had the advantage, but during the night the VC had the advantage. Visibility during the day was a huge benefit for us; we could call in air strikes or artillery when we encountered the enemy. However, during the night we were the vulnerable ones. We could not see the VC moving close to our perimeter, and they could easily pitch a hand grenade or fire mortars on us. The VC would move into the vills at night and confiscate rice while threatening reprisal against the villagers for helping the Americans. I felt sorry for these people. Most would show us hospitality during the day, but by night they had to capitulate to the demands and threats of the VC! I understood their need to do whatever was necessary to maintain their existence and survive.

Sign language was the best way to communicate, so I mimicked washing myself to Papa San. He nodded vigorously and proceeded to pull out a crude bench and put a large basin on the bench. Then he went to a shallow well next to the vill and filled a bucket of water and placed it on the bench. The water table in the delta was very high and a well of only ten to fifteen feet deep provided "reasonably" clean water. I felt a bond toward the old man. He seemed to genuinely care and showed us great hospitality.

Modesty prevailed for Sgt. Powell and me. Although we would have preferred to get naked and wash our entire body, we stripped to our waist and poured the water over each other after we had shaved. It was refreshing, and I felt like a new person.

Nov. 30
And I'm still around
Ha Ha
Ha

Dearest B,
        We had hot turkey yesterday and
everyones moral is much better. We are
and have been on road security between
An Hoa and Liberty bridge since
the 23rd so we may be going into
the bridge soon and have a little
bit of slack time for 5 or 6 days.

        We have been here so long I've
made pretty good friends with this

old papa san in the vill at the
bottom of the hill. When we make
water runs he is right their with a
wash basin and Boo Coq (Vietnamese
for very much) water then he would
sharpen my knife razor sharp, and tell
me with sign language how he
had many relatives in this vill and
in An Hoa and how he cought fish
in basket traps and show me food
like snails and all that. He probably
has a dozen rifles and hand grenades
stached some where also. Oh well
friends by day enemy by nite. What
a shity war.
Now I'm going to go down to papa san
and shave and clean up I'll take
a camera and get a few shots.

Papa San and me in his village

Here comes the water! Sgt. Powell dousing me.

seven

THE SNAKE EYE

While on patrol in the Quang Nam province south of the Song Thu Bon River, we worked our way through a thick stand of elephant grass when my point man spotted an unexploded Snake Eye bomb with its tail fins missing. This was the first time we had come across an unexploded bomb that had not been harvested by the VC. It had hit the ground at a 45 degree angle, and the bomb's nose was buried two feet in the ground. Snake Eye bombs had fins that popped out from the tail of the bomb when released from the F4 Phantom jets that gave us close air support. During close air support we could easily see the fins open up as the bomb left the wing of the fighter jet, often only two or three hundred yards from our lines. The fins acted like a parachute causing the bomb to drag and fall straight down nose first. This allowed the low-flying jet to escape the bomb's explosion. If the bomb's fins broke off, the bomb was defused. This prevented shrapnel from striking the low-flying jet or having the bomb miss the target and land on us. The jet that dropped this Snake Eye had done so at a low altitude and was fortunate the bomb defused. Maybe the fins had been ripped off by a tree or possibly a mid-air collision with the fins of another Snake Eye. Whatever the cause, we now had to prevent a 500 pound explosive from falling into the hands of the enemy.

Because unexploded Snake Eyes were highly valued by the Viet Cong, we had no choice but to detonate it. The VC would harvest the bomb's explosive by using a hacksaw to cut through the casing to get to the "Composition B" explosive (Comp-B). Then they would use the Comp-B to make booby traps. On a previous occasion we had come across a harvested bomb. I looked at the hole cut in the side of the bomb and could not believe the desperate motivation that drove someone to take that risk. There was enough explosive in one bomb to make at least a hundred booby traps. After chipping the Comp-B out, the Viet Cong could easily pack the granular explosive in a tin can mixed with rocks, bolts and screws. Then adding a blasting cap resulted in a lethal homemade booby trap. I was intent on not letting the VC get their hands on this cache of explosive that they could use against us.

The thought of blowing up a bomb made me very nervous. Our demolition training was rudimentary. I knew the mechanics of setting a charge, but there was no formula for how much explosive, C-4, I should use for blowing up this bomb. C-4 is a very high velocity explosive which is good for cutting through steel, but how much would I need to cut through a half inch of steel and ignite the explosive inside the bomb?

We carried at least two or three demolition kits. After all, how could we heat our C-Rations without the C-4 in the demo-kits? The demo-kit came in a canvas satchel the size of a small briefcase. It contained about a dozen bars of C-4 plastic explosive, blasting caps, plenty of fuse and ignition caps to light the fuse. You could also use the flame from a match or lighter to ignite the fuse.

The platoon proceeded on with Sgt. Powell while a few Marines and I stayed behind to set up the demolition. I was thinking, "This has got to work. Pack it with lots of C-4." I took out three bars of C-4 and molded them onto the side of the bomb. They looked like three large band-aids, together about a foot square, plastered to the bomb's casing. Taking the crimping

Graphic of how the large fins of a Snake Eye
Bomb are deployed to slow its descent. Length is 70"

tool from the demo-kit I inserted one end of the fuse, about three feet long, into a blasting cap. I then crimped the cap onto the fuse and stuck the blasting cap into the center of the glob of C-4. Not wanting to fiddle with lighting the fuse with a lighter, I placed an ignition cap on the other end of the fuse. (Ignition caps are also made for igniting a fuse under water.) The ignition cap was a hollow tube the size of an index finger, with a hole in one end to insert the fuse and a pull ring on the other end to activate the spark igniting the fuse.

The burn speed of the fuse was about 45 seconds per foot. So I figured we had about two and half minutes to clear the blast area. This gave us plenty of time to get at least 200 yards away. I pulled the ring on the ignition cap, verified the fuse was lit. Then we hauled ass to catch up with the rest of the platoon. We followed the path the men had laid down through the elephant grass. The path seemed to wind and turn with the terrain. I was totally disoriented by the winding path because we moved fast to get as far away as possible. At about the two minute mark we caught up with the rest of the platoon. I told everyone to get down and we waited. I checked my wrist watch. Two and a half minutes passed. Doubt started to come over me. What if I crimped the fuse too hard and it burned out, was the fuse bad, did the blast cap fall out of the C-4? My doubts turned to fear. I did not want to go back and see what went wrong. Suddenly there was a horrific explosion. The shock wave felt like a blast of wind and the grass bent over us. Our winding and twisting through the grass had not put enough distance between us and the bomb. Everyone was on their belly with their nose buried in the dirt. Fortunately, the thick grass absorbed much of the initial shock, as well as the horizontal shrapnel. The shrapnel that was sent vertically from the blast started to rain down on us. The shrapnel made a fluttering sound like a flag blowing in a stiff wind. It had a low whistling sound as it landed around us. The sound of it hitting the ground was like heavy rocks the size of baseballs. Thank God no one was hit. I would have had a very hard time explaining how someone was wounded from a bomb I blew up.

eight

PATCHWORK OF MEMORIES

The trauma of war creates an indelible mark on your memory. For whatever reason, remembering when something happened seems secondary to the event itself. Many events or brief encounters still remain in my memory of the war. Each event is unique in how it developed, as well as its final outcome. They are not tied together in a sequence nor are they related. Each stands on its own as a day-to-day glimpse of what life was like in the bush. They are like snapshots that swim in my memory as a collage of encounters.

WOMAN AT THE WELL

The village was nestled in trees forming a "V" shape. It was an inviting landscape with the trees on our left and right channeling us into the center of the village. As I looked through my binoculars I could see activity in the vill, a good sign indicating it was unlikely we would get fired upon. As we approached I could see a mama san collecting water from a well.

Suddenly we took automatic fire from the tree line on our left. We approached in the open with little cover so everyone kissed the dirt. Since the fire came from our left side everyone had a clear line of fire into the tree line. Our response was over-whelming; everyone was pounding that tree line with automatic fire. Then a young man dressed in black and carrying a rifle ran toward the village. Everyone's fire followed him into the vill. I could not believe no one brought him down. As he disappeared behind the well the mama san fell to the ground. Why she did not take cover I will never know.

The fire fight was brief, maybe thirty seconds at most. We entered the vill. Mama san was dead. Her gray hair confirmed her grandmotherly status. Younger members of the village showed their grief. They gathered around her rocking back and forth on their knees and wailing in mournful groans. All we could do was move on in hopeful pursuit of the man in black pajamas who fired on us.

This was a classic tactic of the VC. Shoot and then run into crowded civilians hoping our fire would not follow. Then when our fire followed and civilians got killed, it was not the VC who received the blame, it was us! It was clearly a guerilla tactic that worked to their advantage.

Dearest Diana,   Jan. 22
                                  5:00 p.m.
    Last Night we mand a Night move from The Horseshoe to a vill we use to occupy. As we intered The area we were fired upon and we saw the gooks "sky out". So we opened up and Killed Two later The sam Thing happened but a mama-san got in The way and she got it. The march took 14 hrs. and we only came 4 mi. And I'll give you one guess who was point. Yep! me !!

CEASE FIRE!

The chaos of a fire fight is intense. No one more than twenty yards away can hear you yell at the top of your lungs. You just hope everyone uses common sense in where they are shooting.

The heat was intense with the mid-afternoon sun punishing us. The terrain was open as we descended a slow rolling hill toward a wide open rice paddy. Just before we reached the rice paddy a short burst of automatic fire came from a tree line ahead of us. The incoming fire was from over two hundred yards away. It was clearly a burst-and-run situation. We returned fire and a couple of Marines ran down the hill ahead of me and kept firing long after the incoming fire had ceased. I yelled, "Cease fire! Cease fire!" Private Wilson was down the hill fifty yards from me and he kept firing. Then I saw a young boy riding a water buffalo through the rice paddy in front of us. The kid was desperately trying to get out of the line of fire. Wilson was trying to hit that kid! I repeated my call, "Cease fire!" He was the only one who kept shooting. He ejected a clip, loaded another and continued to shoot at the kid who was easily five hundred yards away and whipping the buffalo to go faster. I was certain Wilson heard my command to cease fire when he paused to reload another clip. I did not care if the kid was a VC recruit. I had issued a command and it was being willfully disobeyed. I ran down the hill, ripped Wilson's M-16 out of his hands, threw it to the ground and kicked him squarely in the butt with my right foot and yelled, "Get back to your fire team!" When we got to the top of the hill I threw his rifle in his chest and told him to follow my orders. As he turned and walked away he said, "Don't turn your back on me!" His pride reflected the embarrassment of being reprimanded in front of others and fueled his remarks as well as his anger toward me.

As we set in for the night I reflected on Wilson's response. This was clearly the kind of kid, yes, "kid" at nineteen years old, who could wait for the opportune moment and place a round in my direction during a fire fight. I was not the only one who heard his threat. I could have issued a court martial hearing and had him hauled off to Da Nang on the next resupply chopper, but that was the easy way out and Wilson might have achieved his ultimate goal, to get out of the bush. No, Wilson would be the point man from now on. The point man walked three to four men in front of me. Hence, I would heed Wilson's warning and never have my back to him. The point man was the most casualty-prone position in the bush. The point man would be the first to encounter a booby trap or take fire from a tree line. I was intent on setting an example. After about two weeks we medevac'd Wilson. He tripped a booby trap. Although not life-threatening, his wound was substantial and I made no effort to go to the medevac chopper to bid him farewell.

THE BEST TIME TO MOVE

During the day you could see where you walked. It could be a trail or an opening in some brush or a gap in a tree line. All of these made for prime locations to set a booby trap. But at night you just took a compass heading and walked. The likelihood of hitting a booby trap diminished greatly, because you walked a compass heading, a straight line, which kept you from finding the easy path.

We got the word to move north toward Liberty Bridge. We ate a quick supper and headed out well after sunset. It was a moonlit night with good visibility. The terrain was familiar, and we knew the location of all the vills on our way to the Bridge. It was about 10 p.m. when we entered a vill that was still active with voices. This was not the norm. The VC had moved into the vill during the night. We caught them off guard. We checked all the hooches and found two VC hiding. Then we could hear shouting ahead of us. We had no idea what was being said. We brought the two VC out of the vill with us and planned to ship them to regimental headquarters the next morning for interrogation.

Standing near the shrine where the fire fight started.

It was about midnight when we departed the vill on our way to the Bridge. We had the captives in the middle of our column as we moved past a small shrine that appeared to be a place of worship. The shrine was about six feet high and four feet wide with carved pockets to set offerings and burn incense. All I remember is the sound of bullets ricocheting off the shrine when they started firing at us. We exchanged fire for what seemed a long time, but couldn't have been more than twenty minutes. It was not one or two gooks doing a burst-and-run. It was like they had a mission to pin us down. The exchange of fire was intense. I could not hear the bullets hitting the ground near me. They seemed to be over our heads.

Fortunately there was a C-130 gun ship in our area equipped with Vulcan 20mm cannons. This aircraft was nicknamed "Puff the Magic Dragon," and its ability to cover a football field with deadly fire was impressive. Each cannon could fire thousands of rounds per minute. Puff could not see us in the dark so I rolled over on my back, took out my lighter and flicked it repeatedly until Puff called back confirming he could see our location. Then all I had to say was, "Cover that tree line just north of us." Puff opened up with such a devastating swath of fire, nothing in that tree line could have survived.

We stayed hunkered down for about a half hour. I called for status reports from everyone by word of mouth, up and down the column. Amazingly, no one was injured or hit, but our captives escaped in the chaos of the fight. Upon reflection it became clear to me what had happened. The friends of our captives got out of the vill ahead of us. The commotion in the vill and the shouting must have indicated we had captured two of their companions. In a desperate attempt to free them, they staged an ambush in the hope their fellow VC could slip away during the chaos of the fire fight. I'm sure they purposely fired high to avoid injury to their companions. I'm sad to say their strategy worked and "Puff" strafed a vacant tree line.

HE KICKED UP DUCKS

We hiked south out of the horseshoe heading toward the Bridge. As usual, we had been working through tall elephant grass on a berm overlooking the river and its sand bars. Henderson, my radio man, was only three steps behind me. We could not keep the usual five to ten pace interval while in the tall grass.

Suddenly I heard the splashing of water, flapping of wings and that familiar quack of ducks taking flight. My initial thought was we spooked some ducks off a pool of water below the berm. I wanted to see the event and took two steps toward the edge of the berm. I parted the grass with my hands and to my amazement observed a VC running through a pool of water just below us. He was wearing black shorts, a red shirt and had two bandoliers of ammunition crossed over his back and shoulders. He looked like Pancho Villa.

I kept the grass parted with my left hand as I reached for my .45 pistol in my shoulder holster. I struggled to find the snap to free the pistol. Henderson could see the gook through the grass I had parted. He stepped up with his M-16 over my right shoulder to fire. I did not know he was going to fire. The muzzle of Henderson's rifle was level with my shoulder and about six inches from my head when he fired. I fell to my knees cupping my hand over my right ear. The pain was intense. It was like someone had stuck a sharp pencil deep into my ear. The ringing did not go away for hours. The VC did get away.

DON'T STAY IN THE KILL ZONE!

Maybe it was my training, or maybe I had become hardened by the bush but I adopted that "I don't give a shit!" attitude. Putting ourselves at risk to get out of the kill zone proved to be the right thing to do.

Our training in Marine Basic School was excellent. One course centered on what to do if you are caught in an ambush. Ambushes are well planned. The goal of an ambush is to confine the enemy in a zone of fire and cut them to pieces. This zone of fire is referred to as the "kill zone." The kill zone can be a path with heavy foliage on all sides, or an open space with no cover or egress. The counter-strategy for an ambush is difficult to imagine. One would consider it bordering on insanity, but it works. Since the kill zone is a defined space where the enemy will concentrate their fire, the primary goal is to get out of there as quickly as possible. And the only way to do this is to fight your way out. Our training taught us to initiate a frontal assault toward the direction from which the fire was coming. Everyone is to use full automatic fire holding his weapon at waist level and run directly toward the enemy. Yup, sounds crazy!

I can't remember why we decided to cross a rice paddy adjacent to a small village. It was something I resisted doing unless commanded to get somewhere in a hurry. Nevertheless, it was not a long paddy, a quarter mile across at most. The vill was at our 10 o'clock position and it was only about a hundred yards away when the firing started. It came directly from the vill and was not the usual burst-and-run tactic. The incoming fire was sustained and appeared to be from at least two, maybe three gooks firing. As usual, everyone dove off the paddy dikes into the water and started to return fire. I knew the coordinates of the vill and called in a quick round of artillery, but it missed the vill. There was a brief pause as if they could be reloading. Three other Marines and I jumped up and started to assault the vill. The rest of the platoon quickly followed, firing full automatic and running directly at the vill. We jumped over the dikes and kept running through the paddy water. I'm sure seeing forty Marines running and firing at them gave them incentive to flee.

When we reached the vill it was totally vacant except for a little girl who had been hit in the chest. It was a demoralizing sight. After taking significant fire all we had to show for our effort was a young girl who had no part in the fight. I remember seeing her wound. It was not round, but a flat slit about an inch long as if the bullet had hit her sideways after tumbling from a ricochet. We could find no other signs of blood or wounded. My only thought was, "God, I hate this war!"

On my patrol yesterday we got opened up on and luckly no one was hurt. We were walking across a patty dike and all of a sudden we took automatic weapons fire from the front. I was 5th man back. I never hit the deck so fast in my *life. Right off the dike into the mud and slime, but it felt good. We returned fire and shot some arty at them. This happened two or three times more and then we headed back home. When we started taking fire from a ~~the~~ vill we ~~attayed~~ shot artillery in it and then fired small arms upon intering the only person dead was a 4 yr. old girl. They get rid of the dead enemy so fast. Primarily because of the psycological effect. If you never see what you are killing you get quit frustrated.*

DECEMBER 3, 1968 | IN THE BUSH | TYPESET PAGE 224

HER BREASTS WERE ENGORGED WITH MILK

The vill was not large, maybe four or five hooches. We had no intention of setting up for the night in or near this vill; our objective was to pass through. Our plan to set in for the night was a couple of clicks away.

As we passed by the last hooch in the vill a woman approached me in an urgent manner. It was as if she knew I was the commander of the unit. It concerned me that she could easily identify me as the leader. That recognition as the leader made me the preferred target for a sniper. I took every precaution to avoid being recognized as the person in control. Normally officers in the bush carried only a .45 caliber pistol, but I also carried a rifle to look like everyone else. Maybe it was where I walked in the column, usually 4th or 5th man from point. On second thought, it must have been my radio man who always followed me. That would have been a "dead" giveaway.

She tugged at my arm to get my attention. I took a step back as she pulled open her shirt to expose her breasts. They appeared large and swollen, obviously heavily laden with milk. Her eyes appeared mournful and she was obviously in great distress as she pleaded with me in Vietnamese. I could not understand a word she was saying. My mind raced to try and understand what she wanted. Surely she was not propositioning me in front of my men. She was not malnourished, so begging for food seemed out of place. How I wished I had a Kit Carson Scout to help interpret, but only Company Commanders had access to the Scouts. I'm sure my expression was one of puzzlement mixed with concern. Then I raised my hand with my palm toward her as if to signal, "stop," and I fumbled with one of the few Vietnamese expressions I knew, "khong hieu" (I don't understand). Then I turned and we exited the vill. This event haunted me for some time. Clearly she was proving her motherhood and pleading, or was it shaming. Was she pleading for help for her baby or was she shaming us due to the loss of her baby by virtue of this war. I will never know and ever wonder.

HOW TO CUT DOWN TREES FOR AN AMBUSH

How I loved to blow things up. I think it was the little kid in me. I can remember experimenting with cutting up shotgun shells as a kid to make firecrackers. I would take out the pellets and pack the shell casing with the powder from the shell. Then I'd place a fuse in the casing and light it. It would explode, but not nearly as violent as a cherry-bomb or an M-80, the firecrackers we exploded as kids.

I was totally focused in Basic School during demolition training; learning how to set a charge of C-4, understanding fuse burn rates, crimping blast caps on fuses, and how to use det-cord (explosive cord). Every aspect captured my interest.

But once in the bush there seemed little need to use this skill of demolition other than to blow up an unexploded bomb or set off a booby trap.

Nevertheless, there was a very practical application for demolition: blocking the exit from the kill zone of an ambush. The goal of an ambush is to confine the enemy in the zone of fire. If the ambush is on a trail and trees line the trail, it is ideal to drop a tree at both ends of the kill zone, thus confining the enemy there. That requires setting appropriate explosive charges on each tree at the front and back of the kill zone. So, how do you set a charge that will ensure the tree falls in the desired direction to block the path? It requires setting a "cutter" and "kicker" charge on the tree. The "cutter" charge is placed two to three feet above the ground on the opposite side of the tree from the trail, by hacking a wedge-shaped depression and packing it with C-4. The "kicker" is placed on the same side of the tree about 10 to 12 feet in the air. The "kicker" charge is a round hole about the size of a golf ball, which is then packed with C-4. A string of det-cord is then run from the "cutter" to the "kicker." Finally, an electronic blast cap is placed in the "cutter" with the wire running to a hand-held magneto (hand generator to send electronic charge) and you are all set. Just squeeze the hand-held magneto and the "cutter" charge severs the tree while the force of the "kicker" pushes the tree over in the desired direction across the path.

Oh, how I wanted to deploy this technique on a real ambush, but, alas, our area of operation did not place us in heavily wooded jungle, but rather in rice paddies and tall elephant grass. Nevertheless, I wanted to educate my platoon on this technique. So while resting in the delta on a slow day we found an old tree nearby and I called my squad leaders together for a demonstration. I was feeling a little cocky and quite confident of my skill and training in cutting a tree down with explosives and having it fall in the desired direction. After setting the charges we stepped back a safe distance and I squeezed the hand-magneto. The "cutter" charge completely severed the base of the tree and lifted it a foot straight up in the air - clearly too much C-4. The cutter should not sever the base completely. As the tree came back down on the stump, which now looked like a mass of splintered shards, it slowly tilted in the desired direction. I began second-guessing my men's thoughts, "Yeah, right, the Lieutenant doesn't know how to blow up a tree!" Then it fell to the ground exactly where it was supposed to fall. My pride was saved, and I learned to be stingier with C-4.

FACE TO FACE ON POINT

We started on patrol near the ridge line southeast of the delta far from any villages. It was late evening. Soon it would be time to set up a perimeter for the night. The trail was well-defined and wound in and out of short tree lines. I was fourth man back from point when I heard a burst of automatic fire ahead of me. The fire was not in our direction and then I heard, "Got one! Got one!" As I moved up to the front of the column I could see the trail bend sharply into a tree line. A gook had walked out of the tree line coming face to face with my point man. It was a surprise for both men.

Every point man carried his rifle at the ready with the safety off. The startled gook had no chance. He was carrying an AK-47 and two bandoliers of ammunition crossed over his chest. The point man's burst of automatic fire caught the gook full in the chest. He was clearly in a death rattle as I approached. I could see his legs jerking as life was leaving his body. I said, "I think you need to finish it." Then the Marine placed his M-16 on the gook's forehead and fired a last round. Stillness came quickly. It surprised me to see the flesh on the gook's forehead separate in the pattern of a star, but it quickly made sense after I realized the flash suppressor on the M-16 is shaped with three prongs on the end of the barrel.

It was getting dark and I decided to set in a few yards off the path where the gook was lying. Our perimeter was small with only 10 to 15 yards between positions. At about 2 a.m. all hell broke loose from the direction of the dead gook on the path. Intense automatic fire was spraying our entire perimeter. I could hear the men closest to the trail returning fire. Then I heard one of them take two shots with an M-79 grenade launcher. Although a grenade launcher shoots explosive grenades it can also shoot a buckshot round that is devastating at close range. It was two buckshot rounds that he had wisely used.

The exchange of gun fire stopped abruptly after the two shots from the grenade launcher. We held our position with no one moving or drifting off to sleep for the next two hours. As soon as dawn gave enough light to see, we inspected the location where the dead gook had lain the night before. His body was gone and significant blood trails followed the path where his body must have been dragged. I'm certain the buckshot rounds found their mark.

TOO MANY HAND GRENADES

The net holding our supplies hung low under the CH-46's belly as it gently lowered it to the ground. As soon as the net became slack from the supplies resting on the ground, the net was released and the chopper departed without ever landing. Kelly, our Platoon Guide, started sorting the supplies for distribution to the men. The Platoon Guide is responsible for checking with the men to determine their resupply needs, calling in the supply needs to Regiment and distribute them upon arrival. After sorting through the resupply Kelly approached me with a look of concern, "Lieutenant, this is not our resupply. They dropped some other platoon's supply order on us!" While Kelly and I walked toward the pile of supplies I asked, "What's missing that we need?" "It's not what we need.

It's what we don't need. They delivered two cases of grenades and I did not order any! We can do with the food order and small arms ammo, but not the grenades."

Grenades, although about the size of a baseball, are not light. Each man already carried three to four grenades. It was not practical to ask everyone to load up with three more grenades. The only solution was to destroy them. Rather than set a bar of C-4 on the cases of grenades and blow them up I chose to dispense of them with a training exercise. Learning to throw an air-burst with a hand grenade is tricky business, but essential in the area where we operated. The tall elephant grass greatly diminished the effectiveness of a hand grenade. However, if a grenade exploded above the grass over the enemy's head the casualty radius was much greater.

To throw an air-burst it was necessary to allow the grenade's fuse to ignite while still holding it. This is extremely dangerous and NEVER taught or demonstrated in training. But, what the hell, it was war and we had to improvise in the bush.

The burn rate of a hand grenade's fuse was about seven seconds, give or take a second. We held the safety handle or "spoon" on the side of the grenade and pulled the safety pin. Throwing the grenade would allow the spoon to fly off and the striker to ignite the fuse. No one could throw a grenade far enough to keep it in the air for seven seconds. So, we had to let the spoon fly off while still holding the grenade, count for three seconds and let fly. Holding a live grenade in your hand for three seconds feels like an eternity. Nevertheless, the technique was effective. Everyone practiced throwing air-bursts, but we still had some grenades left over, so I challenged Sgt. Powell to a contest to see who could throw a grenade the farthest. Sgt. Powell threw first and did not release the spoon. I wanted a better grip so I let my spoon fly before throwing. We paced it off and Powell's went 60 yards; mine went 70. My shoulder ached for three days!

DON'T RUN!

He was a long way out in the rice paddy moving away from us. I looked through my binoculars and could see he was of fighting age. If you are fighting age and in the bush, you are going to be hauled in for interrogation unless you have an ID issued by South Vietnam. After having already passed up two other men that walked away from us in a rice paddy and later finding out they were VC, I was not willing to let this guy slip away. He was easily six to seven hundred yards away and that made for an extremely difficult shot for an M-16 rifle. Our sniper team was assigned to another platoon, so I called over one of the M-60 machine gun teams and told them to set up on the edge of the paddy. The effective range of an M-60 is over 1000 yards.

As I stood next to the machine gun team, I cupped my hands and as loud as I could, I yelled, "đến đây" (come here!). He immediately started to run away. I simply said, "shoot him!" The bullets raised pillars of water about 50 yards in front of the running gook and then adjusted on him. He halted and raised his hands and started walking toward us. I was surprised he survived the shower of bullets around him. As he reached the edge of the paddy where I was standing, I saw he had one bullet through the calf of his leg. It was a clean hole that was barely bleeding. "Doc" patched him up and he went out on the next supply chopper. Regimental Headquarters confirmed he was NVA.

Every platoon had its own Corpsman, in civilian terms a paramedic. The Army's term was Medic, but the Marines have no medical personnel so we are assigned a Navy field medic called "Corpsman." Like most platoons we called our Corpsman "Doc."

NICE SHOT!

It was still dark when we moved out. The sun would not be coming up for a couple of hours. I liked moving in the dark since it lessened the chance of hitting a booby trap. We did not walk on defined paths. We just took a compass heading and busted through the brush. But, more importantly, the gooks did not expect us to travel without the security of air power and artillery during the day. It was much more difficult to call in support from aircraft or artillery at night, so night travel put us on more even ground with the enemy. Night movement improved our chances for success to engage the enemy and I was willing to take that risk.

As usual I was 5th man back from my point man as we approached a small vill, only four hooches. I could see the outline of the thatched roofs of the hooches. Then a figure started to run out of the vill. He was dressed in the traditional black of the VC and carrying a rifle. As he mounted one of the rice paddy dikes I opened a hand-held flare, took off the cap that held the firing pin and placed it on the base of the flare. The sharp slap of my palm on the base of the flare sent a bright illumination three hundred feet in the air with a small parachute. The gook was fully exposed and about two hundred yards in front of us. He was running like a sprinter when my point man started firing. To my surprise the firing was not an automatic burst. It was controlled with one squeeze sending each round. Then I saw a tracer from the point man's rifle disappear in the running VC. He fell from the dike into the paddy.

As we moved into the vill, the occupants appeared stoic and resigned to the events that had just taken place. I accompanied a couple of men to the body lying in the paddy. After we pulled it from the muck, I could see a single penetration at the base of his skull just above the back of his neck. It was the best shot I had seen from anyone in the bush.

Dearest Diana.   Jan. 25
11:00

We got up early This morning and hit a village, As we went Toward The vill my point man saw a Gook and killed him he had some NVA uniforms, An AK-47 Assault rifle, chicom hand grenades and magazines for the rifle. We completely checked The vill and found nothing much. Then I put my radio on a frequency which is used by observation planes And had an area observer circle me all The back to the Base camp. Sometimes The field isn't so bad. There is just one Thing wrong with This place! you can get killed. Otherwise, you make mucho $, get a good Tan & OH I forgot one other Thing That Sucks about U.N. being away from you. I guess That is The worst of All.

JANUARY 25, 1969 | IN THE BUSH | TYPESET PAGE 225

HE HAD A HARD-ON

Traveling the ten or twelve miles going north from Liberty Bridge to Da Nang was reasonably secure. We rarely encountered snipers or booby traps. There was no need for an escort when I was called to Da Nang to participate in a court martial of a deserter. It was just me and the driver of the jeep when we left the Bridge in early afternoon.

The road was barely a two lane dirt road with deep ruts and red dust two to three inches deep. We had to cover our nose and mouth each time a vehicle passed us going the other direction. Top speed was twenty to thirty miles an hour.

Just before we reached the perimeter of Da Nang we came upon a lone Marine standing on the side of the road. It was very unusual to see a soldier by himself with no other units or platoons in sight. I told the driver to stop. I wanted to know if this Marine was lost or had a problem and what help we could provide. As the jeep rolled to a stop the Marine was standing next to me. I asked him, "What are you doing out here by yourself?" He paused and looked away as if he was searching for what to say. Then, with a sheepish response, "My buddy is over there," and he pointed to the tall elephant grass about 50 yards off the road. "Tell him to get over here!" He turned toward the grass, cupped his hands to his mouth and yelled, "Duke, you need to get over here. There's a Lieutenant that wants to talk to you." A tall Marine raised himself from the waist deep grass. His back was to us and I could see he was struggling with buckling his trousers. At first I thought he was taking a crap, but as he turned to walk toward us I noticed a young Vietnamese girl rise to her knees with her head barely above the grass. As the Marine walked toward us his erection was still showing through his

In the jeep on our way to Da Nang from Liberty Bridge

trousers. The moment of truth was now self evident. No more questions needed to be asked. His moment of carnal bliss was rudely interrupted and I couldn't have cared less. I fought an urge to smile and forced a stern look of disapproval as he joined his fellow Marine next to the jeep, "Get in the back seat," was all I could say.

As we pulled away I turned and said, "We'll drop you at the Da Nang perimeter, okay?" "That's fine," was the last word from both men. Everyone sat in silence for the last mile of our journey.

BEST LAAW SHOT EVER

We were walking on a slope heading down toward the delta when a VC started running off to the right of us. It happened so fast I don't remember who shot the LAAW.[1] It was about 300 yards away and he was headed for a lone grass-covered hooch. I heard the explosion of the rocket being fired from the LAAW behind me. Just as the gook entered the hooch the rocket hit the structure and it turned into a mass of debris and splinters. Our objective was elsewhere and I had no interest in investigating the outcome. We moved on with no concern for what had taken place. It was just another day in the bush.

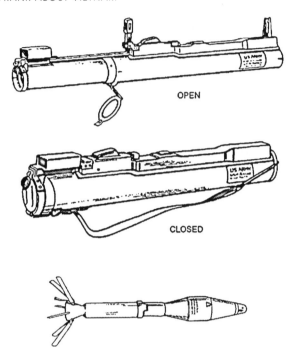

OPEN

CLOSED

1. The LAAW replaced the bazooka, which was a familiar weapon used in World War II. LAAW was the abbreviation for Light Anti-Armor Weapon, a shoulder mounted tube that launched a rocket to disable armored vehicles and tanks. The LAAW was a disposable one-shot rocket, highly portable and was easy to carry since it was a telescoping tube with a 2.75 inch diameter rocket inside the tube. Total length was about three feet once the telescoping tube was extended. The aiming sight popped up when the tube was extended. The effective range of a LAAW was relatively short, only about a hundred and fifty yards. The rocket was designed to penetrate up to eight inches of armor plating.

nine

WHAT'S THE LAAW GOOD FOR?

Early afternoon found us moving through a small village next to a rice paddy. The rice paddy was huge, over half a mile across. Thick jungle surrounded the paddy, which made crossing it an easy target for an ambush from the tree lines. The dikes of each paddy stood two or three feet high above muddy water standing about a foot deep. You could smell the stench of shit from the water buffaloes that worked in the paddies. The paddy looked like a "crazy quilt" that had irregular patchwork, with dikes going every which way. Each dike had a well-worn path on top. I could see green rice shoots rising six to eight inches above the water as I walked on the dikes. It was like walking through a maze to get from one side to the other. We had no reason to cross the paddy and I intended to bypass it by staying in the tree line for better protection. Doing so also gave us the opportunity to move through more villages, which helped understand the villagers' tolerance for our presence. We took note of both friendly and unfriendly vills.

As we entered one of the vills my radio man, Private First Class Henderson, tapped me on the shoulder and held out the radio handset, saying, "Lieutenant, Battalion CP wants to talk to you." I grabbed the handset, pressed the send key and replied, "Delta-1 Actual." Using personal names is a strict no-no. As the platoon commander of Delta Company, 1st Platoon, my call sign was "Delta-1 Actual." The NVA and Viet Cong could monitor our radio frequency, as we could theirs. To give a personal name would give the enemy information they could use to taunt and hinder morale. A common tactic of the enemy was to move as close as possible without detection during the darkness of night and yell, "You chicken shit Marines… come out and fight!" They hoped to persuade one of our positions to return the insult with a burst of fire. Doing so would give away our position and the enemy would have a target to launch mortars or rockets. We also did not want the enemy to have the advantage of using a personal name to taunt us. It would be a bust for morale if they yelled, "Lieutenant Hill, your Marines are chicken shit, come out and fight."

Major Thomas, Battalion Exec Officer, was on the other end of the radio. "We have Charlie Company heavily engaged two clicks (two kilometers) northwest of your location. Get there ASAP!" My response could only be, "Aye, aye, Delta-1 out."

Charlie Company was located on the southern border of the Arizona Territory, named after the badlands of Arizona because it had nothing to offer but kick-ass gooks who didn't give a damn if they died. To get to Charlie Company's location meant crossing that long stretch of rice paddy exposing us during mid-day. There was no time to establish on-call fires on the opposing tree line, so I located a point on the other side that appeared to be the shortest route across the paddy. Then I told my point man to head for that spot. We started out walking on the paddy dikes and separated ourselves by eight to ten paces to limit any casualties from booby traps or enemy fire. As I looked back I could see the forty-plus men following me, stretched out for a quarter mile as we wound around the dikes. Everyone was exposed. Suddenly, automatic fire erupted from the tree line in front of us. We all dove off the dikes into the water. No one was hit. I found myself lying prone in water up to my neck. Mud covered my glasses. I could hardly see. I groped for my map to call in artillery on the tree line that was firing at us. My radio man, Henderson, was next to me and handed me the radio handset. There was little time to identify our location or calculate the coordinates where we needed artillery fire. I struggled with the map and compass to get a fix on our location and identify the source of the fire. Everyone was like me, hunkered down behind a dike and hearing the impact of bullets on the other side of the dike. It seemed like an eternity. I felt so inadequate in our situation. Then Sgt. Powell rose up on his knees, just enough to get his shoulders above the dike. He opened a LAAW (Light Anti-Armor Weapon) and aimed it well above its recommended range. Then he fired it toward the tree line, about 300 yards away.

Some would ask, "Why carry LAAWs when the Viet Cong had no armored vehicles?" We discovered due to the "Munroe Effect" (directional force explosive) we could aim the rocket in front of advancing enemy. Hitting the ground ten meters in front of the enemy resulted in shrapnel, rocks and debris skipping up from the explosion into their faces. It was just like skipping a flat rock across a pond of water. We considered the LAAW instant, portable artillery.

Sgt. Powell's LAAW hit high in the tree line. We could see the explosion above where we saw the gooks shooting at us. Then tree limbs started falling to the ground. Then another Marine fired his LAAW, then a third, then a fourth! It became a chain reaction of Marines firing their LAAWs into the tree line following Sgt. Powell's example. I couldn't have called in a better artillery strike! Within thirty seconds all firing had stopped. The tree line fell silent. One man stood up, then another. Finally we all lifted ourselves out of the muck and back onto the dikes. We walked to the opposing tree line without another shot being fired. We reached the location where Charlie Company was taking fire, but their fire fight had ended. Medevac helicopters had started the process of taking out their

I am firing a LAAW off Liberty Bridge. This is
probably why I have poor hearing in my right ear.

dead and wounded. That night I called in the resupply list for
the next day. I ordered three cases of LAAWs (nine to a case).
Battalion complained about the order for LAAWs, but after
explaining their effective use, they signed off without hesitation.
Every man carried a LAAW and was happy to do so. Then I
wrote a letter to my wife and asked her to send me my contact
lenses. Eyeglasses would hinder me no more.

ten

THE AMBUSH

Dearest Diana,   Dec. 18

        Last nite will be a nite I'm sure
I will relive in a Thousand dreams.
I gunned down a man & woman. They were
undoughtedly V.C. Last nite my plt. and
I recieved an order to set up a nite
Ambush in a region called The Horseshoe,
about a mile and ½ from the Base campe.
The 7th marines were on a big push
so they thought we would get some
as they try tried to make their escape
at nite. I knew the region quite well
having operated in it my first few
days in the bush. We waited until
dark and moved out. The going wasn't

bad at all. We moved 'with' extreme care and quietness. By 8:30 we had reached ~~were~~ our area to set up. It faced North on a 10ft. high sand bar over looking a wide stretch of sand. Behind us tall elephant grass with a small village about 200 meters to our rear. As we set in we ~~heard~~ heard voices and activity from the village. All went well until 05:45 when I was on watch. I happened to look to my left and saw 3 figures walking onto the sand ~~bar~~ bar about 75 meters away. I emediatly got over to the machine gun position and alerted them. My M-16 ~~was~~ ~~on~~ full of Tracer ammo so The Kill zone could be marked by my burst of automatic fire. As they walked closer I moved to the front of my Lines and ~~try~~ Tried to snap off my safty. IT WOULD NOT BUDGE. Then it Klicked off with a noise sent chilles down my spine the 3 figures stopped & crouched for as split second it seemed like eternity then I opened up the light of the tracers made it possible to see the bullets stricking the people. They were so close.

Then my machine guns opened up and all was still. Two bodies lay before us. One got away but left a trail of blood. We stayed in our possitions until the dawn made it possible to go out and pull in the bodies. Two V.C. one a man with over 150ºº in South Vietnamese money and a safe conduct pass through V.C. country. They woman had bandages & rice. They must have been aiding the V.C. No weapons were on the Bodies so I'll always wonder. But all the vietnamese know you don't move after dark or before first light.

They were helping the enemy plus
No civilian runnes around with
that kind of money. After it was all
over I started to shake like a leaf.
What if they would have had weapons
when my safty wouldn't go off.?
Things like that scared the hell
out of me. But it is all over now.
Now I now what it is like to kill a person
un armed in this war. I have no
compashion

compassion. I'm not proud of it but
neither am I resentful of it. I'll
get over it. Most ricky-tick. Well
How have you been! Don't send anymore
vitamines unless I ask for them. I'm
sending a small pair of Binoculars I
borrowed in the field and messed up
so bought them from the man &
just as soon seen them home
as have to hump them in the
field. We are going out to the
bush as a Company tomorrow.
Jeff ████. was sent to the rear.
He messed up and they don't want him

in the field. Now I have got the most bush time of any of the Lts. in the Company!!!! Our new Company Comander is a 1st Lt. if you didn't Know.

This is really a screwed up letter. I dont Know how you will be able to read it. May-be in another 2 or 3 mo. They will jurk me out of the bush as they did Lt. ████. They say Im doing a good job, well I hope that dose not mean more bush Time. Get the bad ones out put the good ones in. If that is the case may-be I should do a bad job. But you know that is not the case. Its possible something like that could cost a mans life. & Then I would have something on my conscence. There is less & less to talk about. I hate to put so much of that junk Like the first of this letter. But that is what I'm doing. Unfortunatly I dont Think anything could make a person more Home sick than war!

over 40 deg's now all I have to do is
last 80 more and it will be close.
How do you write a letter to
someone you miss so much, love
so much and want to see again
so much. It is most difficult
believe me. I wish you could be in
a little bullet proof box and ride
around on my pack so you could
see what I'm doing It is so
strange to have 50 mens lives
in the balance of my decitions.
They come to me for advice on
this & that and it seems so short
a time since I was in their shoes.
The men are great but their
job sucks. They have 13 mo.
of this while officers have 6-7.
We are lucky in many respects while
The Troops get the short end
every Time. And you, you are getting
the short end. But wait till Hawaii
we will see you get the long end
then OK?
          You are the only one.
          Love Hug

The vill was about three clicks (kilometers) east of the Bridge in the Horseshoe and average as vills go. It had about 15 hooches and was a hundred yards south of the river. We had passed through it a few weeks after I took command of Delta-1 platoon. I felt very uncomfortable as we walked on the path among the thatched-roof hooches, checking bunkers and looking for weapons. Unlike many of the vills we had entered where the women took on a humble appearance and avoided eye contact, these villagers looked you in the eye without fear. Their stares appeared as ones of distrust and contempt. Clearly, this was not a friendly vill.

A month had passed and our company commander decided to move on this vill with a hammer & anvil operation. My platoon was chosen to be the anvil, the blocking force, while another platoon pushed through the vill (the hammer). We set up in a line about 200 yards long between the vill and the river waiting for the other platoon to push through the opposite side of the vill to meet up with us.

The Vietnamese had become well aware of how to conduct themselves when Marine patrols moved through their vicinity. Never run! That was a sure sign of hiding something and not wanting to be taken in for interrogation. A person running would get one warning in Vietnamese to "halt and come here," (dừng lại, đến đây), one of the few phrases we memorized. Failure to do so resulted in being fired upon. Anyone caught outside a vill before sunrise or after sunset was considered to be a combatant and fair game.

None of the villages had men between the ages of sixteen and forty. They had either been recruited, willingly or not, by the Viet Cong or they went to Da Nang to find work. In Da Nang they underwent intense questioning by the ARVN (Army of Republic of Vietnam) soldiers and were issued identification cards if they passed the interrogation, or they may have been recruited by the ARVN. Da Nang was controlled by the 1st Marine Division so the chances of being recruited by the VC lessened greatly. Therefore, any young man found in the bush was automatically suspected of being a VC and hauled in for interrogation, or fired upon if he resisted and ran.

The area we occupied for the anvil between the vill and the river was a sandy beach with intermittent berms (twenty to thirty yards apart). The sand wound around the berms and must have been deposited during the monsoon season when the river was running high. Each berm was about five feet high and covered with elephant grass. The berms looked like the top of someone's head sticking out of the sand, smooth on the sides and bushy on top. Lying down on top of the berm in the elephant grass gave good cover and we could stick the muzzles of our rifles through the grass without being seen.

One of my machine gun teams was on a berm to my right as we faced the direction of the vill. We could not see the hooches a hundred yards away through the elephant grass. Then I got a call from the platoon commander of Delta-2, "Delta-1, we are entering the vill." "Copy, Delta-1 out." was my response. Fifteen minutes passed and all was quiet: no shooting, no commotion of any kind. Then two young men dressed in what looked like white pajamas burst through the grass on a berm about fifty yards in front of us. They slid down the berm on their butts and landed on the sand. I yelled, "dừng lại!" (halt!). They did an about face and started to scramble back up the berm. The machine gun to my right opened up. You could see the red tracers disappear in their bodies. Both men slumped to the bottom of the berm, dead.

A brief inspection of their bodies revealed no weapons or documents. However, I was convinced we had just killed two VC or NVA. For me, their actions confirmed it. The enemy never carried weapons during the day because to do so was certain capture or death. They used simple methods to hide their weapons: buried them in bunkers or carve out a depression in a rice paddy dike.

Two more months had passed and our company was

operating in this same location. The 7th Marine Regiment was also working the area. My platoon was sent into the Horseshoe for ambush placement. We set up near the same vill where we had killed the two VC. It was dusk when we moved into position between the river and the vill. I ordered only whispers, no loud talking. The villagers had no idea our location was less than two hundred yards away. There was no cooking by using the plastic explosive, C-4. It had to be a cold supper night. For me it was just a candy bar.

We had established a semi-circular perimeter on a large berm overlooking a long stretch of sand leading to the river from the vill. The tall elephant grass concealed our position well. I placed one machine gun team on the right and the other on the left overlooking the sandy beach. Positioning machine guns on the left and right flanks allowed for crossing fire, the preferred setup for an ambush.

The sky in the east was turning a deep purple with hints of orange. It would be thirty minutes before the sun peered over the grass. As I looked southeast where the vill was located, I saw three figures on the sandy beach. All I could make out in the dim light over the elephant grass was their cone-shaped hats. They came around a berm and started walking on the sand right in front of us! Although still over a hundred yards away they continued to walk toward us. So, I crawled over to my machine gun team to my right. They had fallen asleep, but I alerted them quietly. My intention was to get closer and challenge the three to halt. I grabbed my M-16 rife with a full clip of tracers.[1] I did not want to stand and expose myself, so I crawled down the slope of the berm to the sand. I knelt just inside the grass and lifted my M-16. I fumbled for the safety. The three figures now passed in front of me only sixty yards away. I flipped off the safety. I'll never know if it was the click of the safety or if I rustled the grass that alerted them. They spun around toward me and crouched in a threatening manner. I could not tell if they had weapons in the dim light. I panicked and failed to challenge them to halt. I was not willing to wait while they crouched. I fired on full automatic emptying all twenty rounds in my clip. The steady stream of tracers seemed to envelop them and two dropped immediately. The third ran for the opposite bank and disappeared in the grass. My fire awakened everyone. The machine gun on my right opened up and sprayed the two left lying on the sand. I watched in a moment of suspended animation. For the first time, by my own hand, I had just killed two individuals. I regretted not having issued a challenge. I started second guessing myself, thinking, "I could have challenged them. That would have awakened everyone." It was over in a blink of an eye. I did not want to witness what I had done by viewing two people I had just killed. Two of my men went to the bodies and took all their personal belongings. One man called back and said one was a woman and the other a man, both unarmed. My heart sank as I thought, "I just killed a woman and a man! Were they VC or innocent civilians?" I did not know. A numbness of uncertainty come over me. We left the bodies on the sand. The villagers would certainly pick them up and bury them.

It was about two weeks later that I heard from intelligence that the documents my men had recovered from the bodies confirmed them to be North Vietnamese infiltrators. They had Vietnamese currency (Dong) worth $150. This was far more money than the average peasant of the area would carry. The most probable explanation was that money was intended to pay VC recruits. They also had personal letters from North Vietnam. Although this information gave me some relief, the fact that I had killed an unarmed woman distressed me greatly. It would haunt my conscience for years to come.

1. The reason I carried only tracers was to define the kill zone. A tracer is a bullet with phosphorus packed in the tail of the bullet. When fired, the phosphorus ignites and burns bright red making the trajectory of the bullet visible. Every forth bullet of machine gun ammunition is a tracer. However, having only tracers in my clip made my line of fire extremely visible to the men in the platoon.

As the platoon commander, I was in contact with my fellow platoon commanders and knew the location of their units while doing coordinated maneuvers. If we encountered fire, I would fire a burst of tracers to the left and then another burst to the right and my platoon would then know they needed to confine their fire between my two bursts. Only my platoon sergeant or I carried clips filled with tracers.

eleven

CHRISTMAS EVE WASN'T FUN

Dearest Diana   Dec. 24

    I hope this letter gets to you before the man in "Blue" YES! Ive been wounded. Most Lucky to still be around. The wound is not serious at all a piece of shrapnel went through The back of my flack jacket and just cut the flesh. Nothing to worry about. They just put a band-Aid on it and that was all. I wont even be Taken out of The Field so you know it is not serious.

We were on patrol this morning when I must have tripped a booby-trap. All of a sudden it exploded between me and my radio man. He got the worst of it. Shrapnel all over his body. I was about 10ft.

Away and the blast just stunned me and knocked me off my feet. At the same time I felt this hot burning in the middle of my back. A small piece about the size of a match head went through the flack. If I hadn't of had it on it would have put a hole thru me most likely. Two more and I go out of this Country. I'll settle for no more and make it home in a few extra months. Well here it is Xmas Eve and it sure doesn't seem like it here. But how could it out here. The truce starts at 1800 Today & ends at 1800 Tomorow on the 25th I Think Tonite They will Break it. It seems strange but having grenades go off 10 & 15 yds away is getting to be common place. Every time my plt does SOMETHING it gets hit or hits something. Never will I be so Thankful as Today. It is too bad my radio man was hurt so badly. He had shrapnel all Through his bod, both Legs & Arms and Neck.

There must be something I can talk about other than this ~~fucking~~ war.

DECEMBER 24, 1968 | IN THE BUSH | TYPESET PAGE 228

Christmas Eve, 1968. We had just finished a short layover at Battalion Headquarters. Everyone loaded up on treats to take back to the bush for the holiday. My radio man, Henderson, strapped on a full case of Coke in addition to his radio and backpack. I couldn't believe he could carry a case of Coke on top of the radio. The radio was the size of a brief case and his pack hung below the radio. The addition of that case of Coke made him look like a camel. Henderson was short and stout and the additional load did not seem to faze him. I was happy with a few Snickers bars in the pocket of my flak vest. I craved Snickers and they made for a special treat.

No one was looking forward to spending Christmas Eve in the bush. Everyone was in a bad mood as we headed south from Liberty Bridge, but the Cokes and candy took some of the edge off. We planned to find a spot to set up for the night near a vill we knew was friendly. Having the VC test our lines with taunts and grenades on Christmas Eve was not something we looked forward to and being near a friendly vill lessened the chance.

The terrain was low, rolling, brown grassy mounds with green patchy tree lines. I relaxed a bit when I could easily see into the tree lines; it seemed to lessen the threat of getting fired upon since VC always wanted dense cover. Nevertheless, we moved in single file with five paces between us. I was never more than three or four men behind my point man. Henderson always followed me with the radio. The antenna was bent over and strapped to the side of the radio, making it difficult for gooks to identify the radio man and thus the platoon leader in front of the radio man. Both Henderson and I would be considered prime targets for snipers.

85

We walked on a narrow path, no more than a foot wide. Grass covered it frequently. Not passing through thick brush or trees, our concern for booby traps relaxed. A middle-aged woman was squatting about twenty feet off the side of the path. She faced us with her arms resting on her knees and the tails of her black shirt resting on the ground. I noticed that her teeth showed black stains from chewing betel nuts, a mild stimulant from the Areca palm. She was not alarmed and seemed to go about her business as we passed. As she rose and walked away it was clear what she was doing. She was taking a crap! No one laughed or commented on the casual nature of a woman relieving herself on the side of a path while a line of soldiers passed by her. At the time I gave it no more thought than if I saw a dog crapping. We did the same thing, but now forty-three years later and reflecting on the sight of a woman doing it so casually, confirmed my feelings at the time that modesty was not an issue for us. We had definitely adapted to the social norms of this land.

We pressed on. Suddenly a loud blast lifted me up and threw me forward face down on the ground. It was like a car hitting me in the back. My ears started to ring like crazy and I lay there for just a few seconds trying to collect my senses. Henderson took the full force of the explosion in his face. I felt a burning sensation between my shoulder blades, but the burning lasted only a few seconds. Although the blast disoriented me, I was able to get to my feet. I turned around and saw Henderson flat on his back writhing in pain. Some of the soda cans he was carrying spewed their contents as if a cork had popped off a bottle of champagne. Doc was there in a flash. Although Doc was short and portly, he could move like a rabbit. He usually walked in the middle of the column so he could respond in both directions, front or back of the column. Upon surveying Henderson's puncture wounds it was clear the blast came from a hand grenade. It was one of our hand grenades. How the VC got them I'll never know. The puncture wounds

Sitting on my "rubber lady" with my flak vest and a pen
stuck in the hole where the shrapnel penetrated the vest.

reminded me of a shotgun blast. Henderson's legs had multiple
puncture wounds and his face took three or four fragments.
Each fragment was about the size of a sunflower seed.

Our hand grenades are not necessarily intended to kill, but
rather wound. Think about it. War is focused on attrition. If you
kill the enemy, he gets buried and his comrades continue on. If
you wound the enemy, someone has to care for him, someone
has to transport him, he takes up space in a medical facility. It
requires time, effort, and money to restore him. All this is a
drain on the enemy's capability to fund and support the effort.
Yes, wounding is better than killing! Our hand grenades had
improved considerably from World War II where the outer
casing had deep grooves creating half inch squares of shrapnel.
Our grenades had a smooth outer casing and behind the casing
was a thick wire wrapped around the explosive core. That wire
resembled a spring. It was notched every quarter inch so it

would break apart and create a small piece of shrapnel - like the pellets from a shotgun shell. These little bits of shrapnel far outnumbered the shrapnel from the grenades of World War II and greatly extended the effective casualty radius of the explosion. (Diagram in Appendix)

I could only assume I screwed up and tripped the booby trap. I felt responsible for what had happened. How stupid could I have been? But I felt nothing on or under my foot. The explosion was just a few feet behind me, which seemed too soon for the normal 7-second fuse on a grenade. Grenades have a striker that makes a snapping sound when it ignites the fuse. So how come I felt or heard nothing? In retrospect there can only be one explanation. The spoon-striker-fuse-blast cap assembly was one unit that could be unscrewed and removed from the grenade, exposing a small well into the core of the explosive. A wired blast cap could then be inserted in the well of the grenade and the wire buried underground to a remote location. A VC observing our movement could then instantly explode the grenade by a simple squeeze of a hand-held magneto (a small generator capable of delivering an electrical shock to ignite a blast cap). The perfect place to explode a grenade would have been between a platoon commander and his radioman.

Doc ripped off Henderson's trousers to expose his thighs and lower torso. Henderson took multiple hits on the thighs and his penis was bleeding from one side that was sliced open. It looked like something took a bite about the size of a quarter out of it. I felt a chill run down my spine and dropped my head in sympathy as I turned away to get the radio for calling in a priority one medevac. Henderson was a valued companion in the bush. He was always there handing me the radio when I needed it. He never complained about being targeted as the Lieutenant's radio man. Upon reflection, I thought, "The wire shrapnel could not have caused that much flesh injury, so it must have been the metal casing on the grenade that sliced off the side of his penis."

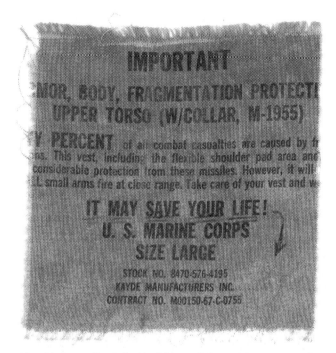

I had to save the label inside my flak vest as a souvenir.
The arrow points to the shrapnel hole. I think God intended
the hole to be an exclamation point as well!

Henderson's wounds did not appear to be life-threatening, but the extent of the multiple penetrations qualified for a priority one medevac. After Henderson was airlifted and on his way to Da Nang, I learned Doc called in the casualty report. He included me as being hit with the booby trap. It was not a big deal as the shrapnel from the grenade sliced through the flak vest between two protective layers of bullet proof plates. Each plate was about five inches square and they overlapped like the outer skin of an armadillo. The small piece of shrapnel was mostly spent by the time it penetrated my flak vest and came to rest just under the skin. I had hurt myself worse shaving! Doc removed it with a small cut and tweezers. No stitches, just some antiseptic and a band aid. The most interesting aspect of this encounter was that the shrapnel passed through the patch on my flak vest where, ironically, it said, "IT MAY SAVE YOUR LIFE!"

twelve

CAPTURING NVA OFFICER

Dearest Diana,   13 Jan.

     Well, here we are over the 3 mo. mark starting #4. A lot has happened or I should say I have got some news since the tape. As for the tape you can send one back if you want but don't buy a recorder because there is plenty in my plt. Their not going to get me babe; they can't do it; I'm too mean.

     More news! Would you believe that I have more bush time than all the other plt. Commanders in the BN! (Battalion) that means if no one gets bumped off I'll be the next to get pulled out of the bush.

That means about one more Mo. in the bush, and right. in the middle of the worst time, TET! But Like I said we're going to make it, We are all rested up and ready to go. We will be moving into the "HorseShoe". They have ~~bin~~ been bombing the hell out of it and the New Jersy has been shelling the area also. We will be moving into the "shoe" on the 16th it will last a few days and then we will probably move south and operate.

Guess Who is point for that nite move into the shoe! yup me. Well it guess we should be. After all I have the best plt. I have been stedily improving my short timers stick. Now I've put a 50 calibre point on it. It helps quite a bit at nite. keeps me from runing into obstucals or falling into holes. Boy!

JANUARY 13, 1969 | BATTALION HEADQUARTERS, LIBERTY BRIDGE | TYPESET PAGE 228

Dearest Diana   Jan. 20 th

We have been on an OPERATION now
for five days. That is one of the reasons
I have not had the time to write. Today
we have a little slake time while the
ARVN's push toward us. Bad NEWS!
our Captain was injured pretty badly yesterday
he stepped on a booty trap. He got shrapnel
all over his body and in his elbow. He
won't be back! Most likely he will be
in the rear or sent back to the States.
I've been a little sick the past few nites
I have the runs and puked a few times
last night. I'm feeling somewhat better
to-day though and I'm loseing wt. The
heat is a bitch. I'm sure getting sick of
this shit. And the worse is yet to come! "TET"
The first few days of this OPERATION we captured
a communications officer and many maps and
inteligence for TET. My platoon did the greater
part of it. We killed about 6 gooks that
day also. Well! I heard today that those one
or two LTs that were ahead of me have now
left the bush. I sure wish they would get

to me. One way or the other I'm not going to return to the bush after R & R. So. don't worry! I will have already had mucho time too I should not kick tho! the grunts have to put in 13 mo in the bush. I can't see that. Maybe they can understand the pressure. Sometimes I think I'm going off my rocker. I hate to send this letter since it is so depressing. because I sure am down in the dumps. Well, maybe things will look up in March. I think you are right those packages probably went down with that plane. So send a few more oysters, Artichokes ect. If you don't mind I guess I'm going to need a few more watch band pins after all. the other day one of my men was burned and as I threw off my flack gear ripped off my watch. So send a few more. What is this about you gaining wt? Why do you have to see a doctor about your wt? How much do you weigh? You arn't sick are you? Take care of yourself for Crists sake after all, you are all I have. Or I should say all I EVER WANT! OH, HUM!, absence make the heart grow fonder. See what you do for me just sitting here talking to you makes me feel better. I love you.

Captain Gilson had been our company commander for a couple of months. He was one of the best commanders I had ever served under. He was slight in stature and had a swagger that let you know he was in command. Never did he mince words. Gilson told you what he expected and I, as well as my fellow platoon commanders, did not argue. During my time in the Marine Corps I had come to recognize someone who knew how to lead.

My health and weight were returning. I clearly recall the turning point. Through worry and anxiety I had almost wasted away. Then I made a conscious decision, "Catching a bullet was better than what I was experiencing, so to hell with it. If it's going to happen, it will and there is no sense in worrying about it." That turnaround in my attitude as well as Captain Gilson's leadership style helped me regain my strength and ability to effectively lead my men.

It was early in the morning on a cloudy overcast day when Gilson called me and the other two platoon commanders into his headquarters' camp site. He laid out a plan for a "hammer and anvil" movement into what we called the Horseshoe of the Song Thu Bon River. This river was like the Mississippi, lazy-moving and muddy with swirling eddies as it wound its way through the northern delta. The distance from shore to shore was two or three hundred yards, making crossing possible only by boat or bridge. It was an old river with large sand bars. At home we called these sand bars "oxbows." When a river swells and deposits sand and then recedes as it winds around the next bend it leaves an "oxbow."

Captain Gilson's plan was well conceived. The river in the Horseshoe provided a natural containment for the enemy. If one platoon could maneuver to the top of the Horseshoe during the night and establish a defense line (the anvil) ringing the top of the Horseshoe, the other two platoons would push through the base of the Horseshoe (the hammer) and push the enemy into the platoon at the top. Using geological features like rivers and mountains to aid strategy by confining the enemy made a lot of sense.

I had established a reputation for accuracy as a good navigator with a compass and map. Although proud that Captain Gilson chose me and my platoon to navigate through the night and establish the anvil (containment line) at the top of the Horseshoe, I tried to hide a feeling of anxiety. I was not looking forward to this night march. Although the distance was relatively short, only four to five clicks (kilometers), it was through heavily populated villages and low level marshland. The elephant grass in the Horseshoe was thick and high, reaching over our heads in many places. It would not be possible to see features like villages or hills to aid our navigation. Estimating the distance covered and using a compass would be the only way we could make this night march. Delta-2 and Delta-3 platoons would be the hammer and start their push toward us at dawn.

The sun faded and we saddled up with our packs. We had a half moon, which helped with close movement. The elephant grass was worse than I expected. It made visibility impossible for more than three feet. We could not keep the five to ten-pace interval between us to limit casualties from booby traps. Our interval was one arm's length apart. It was so dense that a hand grenade could go off just feet away and the grass would absorb all the shock and shrapnel.

During daylight operations and with clear terrain I was usually the third or fourth man from my point man. We always travelled in single file forming a column. The lead man in the column, point man, was not a desirable place to be since that position was usually the first to attract enemy fire or trip a booby trap. My new radio man was right behind me so I could be in instant contact with Battalion Fire Control. By being close to my point man, it was usually easy to give guidance to him. This was not the case on this night. We had to move as quietly as possible and no commands could be given. I took the

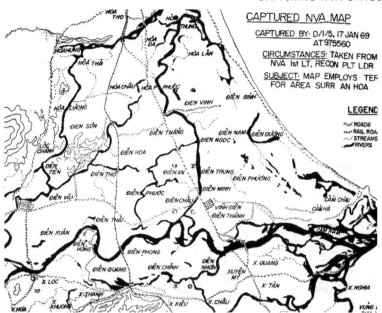

Replica of the map taken from the NVA officer we captured.

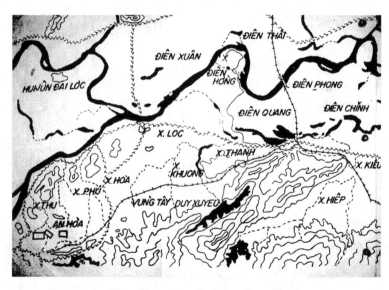

Close-up of the "Horseshoe" on the Song Thu Bon River.
The line in the Horseshoe depicts the approximate route my platoon took
to the top. You can see the line close to the village Dien Hong where VC
called out their challenge.

position of point man with compass and map in hand.

It was slow going, about one click each hour. We hit a swamp that was waist deep and 30 yards across. The mud grabbed our boots and sucked them down six inches into the muck. Every step was like pulling up ten pounds on your foot. The leeches slipped up our pants and attached to our legs, but there was no time to remove them. We had to move on. Besides, weren't leeches used as a health remedy in the 1600s?

We skirted a vill about 100 yards to our left. They must have heard us. How they heard us was a mystery to me. All I could hear was the soft rustle of the elephant grass from the Marines following me. Then there came a taunt from the vill, "Hey, you fucking Marines, come out and fight." No doubt this was the only English the gooks knew and probably given to them by the NVA. By now this was a common taunt we had become immune to hearing. Our movement became more subdued. The taunters had no idea of our intention and every man's discipline kept us from responding. They would get their wish in the morning.

The sky in the east was turning a deep purple with hints of orange when we reached the top of the Horseshoe. We deployed in a battle line with each man in sight of the other. We set in from five to twenty yards apart. We had our backs to the river with our focus on the terrain in front of us. Within an hour we could hear sporadic shooting. It was not a pitched battle where the shooting was a constant roar, but rather skirmish fire with a burst of automatic fire every twenty to thirty seconds. Two Viet Cong broke through our line and dove into the river to swim to the other side. Why they did not get fired upon before getting to the river I will never know. I can only guess the grass was so thick they broke through before anyone could engage them. Their effort was in vain. Automatic fire raked both after swimming only twenty yards from shore. Their lifeless bodies floated head down past our position.

Delta 2 platoon was the first to reach our position. Surprisingly, most of the fire fight took place as they moved through the vills to our location. Then we heard a call from one of the men from Delta 2, "I got a gook, I got a gook down here." I rushed to the location and observed a man in the fetal position cramped in a small depression dug out against the bank of the river. He had already been relieved of his weapon, a 9mm pistol. He had a small cloth bag filled with rice and a leather satchel. He appeared frightened, but was non-compliant to our commands to come out of the depression. Clearly, he did not understand our demands.

I radioed Captain Gilson and told him we had captured a gook. He replied, "I'll be there in ten minutes." Captain Gilson showed up with his Kit Carson Scout, a converted Viet Cong. The Scout was one kick-ass dude. The Kit Carson Scout grabbed the prisoner and pulled him out of his depression in the bank while yelling in Vietnamese. I was standing there wondering what the hell was going to happen next. Captain Gilson was forcefully asking the Scout to get information from the prisoner. Gilson was asking for his unit, location and force strength. The prisoner assumed a position with his knees drawn up to his chest, his head between his knees and he was non-responsive. Gilson pulled out his 45-pistol and pulled the slide back, loading a bullet into the chamber. Then he put the muzzle of the pistol on the prisoner's big toe. I was standing there in amazement and thinking, "Holy shit, he's going to blow off this guy's toe." I really didn't care, but I was in a state of suspense. Then Gilson told the Scout, "Tell him for every question he does not answer, I'm going to blow off a toe." It was amazing how fast the prisoner started to spill his guts and answer every question from the Kit Carson Scout. I don't know if Captain Gilson would have pulled the trigger. It might have been a bluff, but it worked and the gook saved all his toes. The contents of his satchel provided a map of the area and credentials that confirmed our prisoner was an officer in the NVA.

thirteen

FRAG YOURSELF

The chopper lifted off with the NVA officer we had captured along with Captain Gilson's Kit Carson Scout. The Scout was needed to help with interrogation of the prisoner at Division Headquarters.

It was late morning and we had plenty of time to develop a strategy for our next maneuver. Captain Gilson was not interested in coordinating another plan that involved all three platoons of Delta Company. Instead, he directed us to move south out of the Horseshoe and keep at least two clicks between platoons. This was our usual search and engage strategy. We moved through the area checking out vills for weapons, looking for booby traps, and drawing occasional sniper fire just by showing our presence. Most of the time the sniper fire was what we called a "burst and run." One or two Viet Cong would empty a clip at us from a remote tree line and then run like hell. They knew our firepower would overwhelm them if they stayed to fight.

The thick elephant grass in the Horseshoe made movement slow and laborious. After traveling about 4 clicks it was late afternoon. We needed to start looking for a good place to set up for the night. We had to stop on the east side of the Horseshoe, near the river, and had not passed through a single village. We came upon what appeared to be the berm of an old railroad bed. The berm followed the contour of the river and was about 4 feet high and stretched for as far as we could see. We could stand on the berm and see a couple of miles across the Horseshoe. It was as flat as a pancake. The only thing taller than a man was the elephant grass. After inspecting the berm more closely it appeared to be a long running dike to protect the interior of the Horseshoe from flooding. Regardless of its function it provided the best cover from enemy fire in the event the Viet Cong decided to probe us during the night.

There was no point in setting up a circular perimeter. Doing so would create too much risk of firing on each other due to the limited visibility of the elephant grass. Forming a straight line on the river's side of the berm gave us good visibility over the grass to see movement and the river gave us protection from enemy movement from our rear.

Everyone dropped their packs and started to prepare their positions for the night. Some dug in while others just relaxed on the berm. The river was less than twenty yards behind us and many of the men had trampled down a path to the river to fill their canteens and take a quick dip in the water to cool off. The location seemed so isolated and risk-free that no one wore their flak vest or helmet to walk the twenty yards to the river. I no longer complained or chewed anyone's butt for not wearing their helmet or flak vest. I trusted each man's discretion for self-protection given the situation and this location seemed stable.

Suddenly there was an explosion along the path everyone was using to walk to the river. The explosion was followed by screaming, "Corpsman, Corpsman!" I followed Doc to the source of the screaming and watched while he attended to a Marine named Davis. I asked a couple of the men who accompanied Davis on the trail, "What happened?" Their response seemed hesitant and uncertain. "I guess he hit a booby trap, Lieutenant," one of them said. "But everyone has been walking this path for the last hour," I replied with a tone of suspicion. Then I noticed Davis had his helmet and flak vest on. My suspicion started growing and I looked directly at Davis' two companions and asked, "Did Davis frag himself?" Both men failed to maintain eye contact with me and stammered, "Ahhh… no, Lieutenant, I don't think so." I knelt down next to Doc while he was working on Davis. Davis was clearly in shock and took on that pale ashy appearance. By now I was convinced he had fragged himself. I asked Doc, "How bad is it? What priority medevac is needed?" (Corpsmen determine the severity of the wounded and the priority for medevac. Priority 1 is urgent, life threatening. Priority 2 is stable, but evacuate as early as possible. Priority 3 is non-life threatening and evacuation can occur on the next resupply chopper.) Doc replied, "It was a hand grenade. Most of the shrapnel is in the butt and lower legs, but one fragment caught him above the belt in the lower back." "What's his priority?" I barked. "Certainly a 2, but could be a 1." Doc replied. Doc could sense the anger swelling in me.

Davis had at least one, maybe two previous Purple Hearts. I can't remember for sure. For whatever reason the policy in Vietnam was to rotate soldiers back to the states if they incurred three separate wounds (Purple Hearts). I felt this was an incredibly stupid policy. Once a soldier got one or two legitimate wounds the stress of fighting gave them serious thought for self-inflicting a third wound. I despised this policy and could not understand why a rule of warfare like this was in place.

By now it was clear to me what Davis had done. I had heard from other platoon commanders about a method used by some to self-inflict a wound. They would put on a helmet and flak vest. Tilt their helmet back to protect the back of their neck. Then they would reach down and grab their balls and pull them up with their hands cupped to protect them. Finally, they would pitch a grenade 6 or 7 feet behind them. The helmet & flak vest protected the vital organs and their butt and legs would get peppered with some shrapnel. Unfortunately for Davis, when he grabbed his balls his flak vest lifted up above his belt and he took a piece of shrapnel in the lower back. Doc couldn't tell if the small piece of shrapnel caught a kidney or other vital organ.

I leaned down and grabbed the collar of Davis's flak vest. Although in shock he was well aware of what was happening. With as much intensity as I could muster I barked, "You chicken shit son-of-a-bitch! I know you fragged yourself and you're going out as a priority 2 medevac and if you die, it's your own fault." I made certain Doc and Davis's two companions heard my response.

I stood up and stormed back to the berm. I called for my radio man. "Give me the radio!" I commanded. Then I walked far enough away so no one could hear me and called in a priority 1 medevac. As far as I know, after my display of anger, no more self-inflicted wounds occurred in the platoon. At least, for sure, no one attempted a "self-fragging."

fourteen

GOODBYE BYE, YOU'RE A GOOD MAN

Sergeant Powell had to be medevac'd as a result of wounds from a booby trap in January. He had taken a lot of shrapnel from a grenade in his shoulder and spent ten days in intensive care. I felt a deep loss to see Sgt. Powell leave us. I relied heavily on his bush experience when I first arrived. Officers might not want to admit it, but we rely heavily on our platoon sergeants. Sgt. Powell was my right hand man.

Our platoon was down to fewer than thirty men and the most senior enlisted man after Sgt. Powell was Lance Corporal Bye. It seemed unreal to me that the second in command of a platoon in combat would be a Lance Corporal, but this was war in the bush and attrition had taken its toll. Whoever had the guts, drive and knowhow was the best to lead. Bye had them all. Although Bye was not the only Lance Corporal in the platoon, I chose him to replace Sgt. Powell.

Robert was Bye's first name, but everyone called him by his nickname, Skip. I liked Skip a lot. He had a free-spirit attitude and was fearless. He was young, maybe twenty, and in great physical shape. He followed orders without question and led his fire-team with the confidence and respect of every man. After Sgt. Powell left, Skip and I bonded and led the platoon together.

On one occasion we got a welcome surprise in the bush.

A resupply chopper delivered two cases of beer with our regular order for resupply of ammo and field rations. The beer was warm, but wonderful! Every man got one or two beers and we shared cans of peanuts. Skip and I enjoyed a beer together in an abandoned vill.

Skip (right) and I enjoying a beer in the bush.
I'm sad to say this is the last picture taken
of a valued brother in combat.

Feb. 3   4:30 p.m.

Today was my worst in Vietnam to date. One of my best men died Today. We were making a night march and I was point as usual. We intered This hill and gooks Took off running. We opened up Killing 3 and captured 3. We decided to search out The area and found rockets and medical supplies. We continued to search and 8 man from 3rd plt. hit a white phosphorous booby-trap resulting in very serious burns on his legs. We decided there must be something important if they booby traped that tree line. So about five of us decided to go in and check it out. Then some thing else occupied my attention and The others went on. All of a sudden There was This massive explosion. I knew imediatly what it was and knew they were all killed. Skip Bye The boy I lost stepped on a 155mm Cannon shell. I couldn't look at the body I just heard what it Looked like and I'll leave it at that. He was an outstanding marine

and did a fantastic job in place of
Sgt. Powel. I Thank God I wasn't
with him. I'm so sorry for his wife he
just had a baby girl two weeks ago
and for the first time in a long time
I weeped like a baby. I'm really scared
Diana, I've had so many close calls. I
sure hope I don't have to go back
to the bush after R & R. I know I
won't feel Like it, I feel so strange right
now. I'm alive I can see, feel, breath and
Taste, for WHAT? Why? What is life?
something that should be valued so much!
He felt no pain! Yet just 5 minutes
before he died we were laughing and joking
arround. May be that is why it hit me so
hard at first. I guess I'm not as hard as
The outside looks. Today I'm sad, I can't write
a happy letter so I'll close. I'm sorry if you
are sad Now. I'll do my best to make you
Happy in Hawaii. Diana, Thanks for the
pics They are Number one, I love you so much.

your Loving
Husband
for ever & ever
Frank.

fifteen

CHANGE OF COMMAND

Captain Gilson, our company commander, had been severely wounded from a booby trap and evacuated. My platoon and I headed to Liberty Bridge to meet our new company commander, 1st Lieutenant Riner. I guess Captains had become in short supply now that we had a 1st Lieutenant as our company commander. Other companies had 1st Lieutenants as their company commanders so it was not surprising to see Riner take over. He had seniority, more time in grade, than the rest of us Lieutenants. The Marine Corps was rigid in assigning command positions when it came to seniority.

I recall Riner as tall, 6'3", fair complexion with blond hair. If you walked by him on the street you would think he was a big dude from Sweden. He hailed from the Midwest and spoke with what I thought was a southern twang. He appeared to be detached and somewhat aloof. This was his initial tour in Nam and he had no bush experience. That did not matter in the Marine Corps. Anyone completing officer's basic infantry training was considered capable of leading troops in combat.

Right off the bat you could tell Riner was going to prove himself and, by golly, he would get respect through his command presence. He seemed overly confident and apparently not interested in hearing my, or any of my fellow platoon commanders' opinions on our area of operation, the location of friendly vills or where we had the worst fire fights. He was only interested in following the book and kicking some gook ass.

The next morning Riner brought me and my fellow platoon commanders together to lay out the plan of operation for the next few weeks. The plan was to work the area southeast of the Bridge doing the standard search and destroy operation, search for weapons caches, destroy them and hope to encounter some gooks. I was very familiar with this area. Company commanders had to pick which platoon they would travel with while on maneuvers. Riner chose my platoon. By now I had more time in the bush than my fellow platoon leaders. I suspect that is why he chose to be with my platoon. I was not thrilled. I was already beginning to question his ability to command.

Pointing to his map, Riner said, "We're going to head south on this road and jump off here. Then we will move through this vill. I plan to prep the vill with 81mm mortars as we leave the road." He wanted to follow the "book" and prepare the enemy-held position with heavy bombardment before assaulting the enemy's position. I recognized the vill Riner was pointing to on the map. It was the same vill where we had killed the water buffalo a couple of months ago. My mind flashed back to that moment and the faces of the villagers. I told Riner, "This is a friendly vill. I've been through it and never taken any fire. Why not position the mortars to fire on the vill if we take fire from them? You know, set up an on-call fire." "NO! This is the way we're going to conduct this movement," was his response. His head dropped to view the map and he avoided eye contact. His arms straightened as he looked down at the map and he lifted his head saying, "This is the way we will conduct this operation!" I had clearly questioned his judgment in front of my fellow platoon commanders. Not a good way to start a trusting relationship with your commanding officer.

We headed south from the Bridge. My platoon was in the lead. As usual I was 4th man back from my point man. Riner was in the middle of the column with his radio man. We walked in fresh tire tracks from a recent convoy. That made it easy to see a booby trap. If the track was broken or covered over, watch out!

As we left the road I began hearing the explosions ahead of us. We wound around the rice paddies in the tree lines and I could catch a glimpse now and then of the mortars hitting the village. I lost count of the number of rounds that exploded. I would guess at least twelve mortars hit what I considered a friendly vill. I hoped the villagers could get inside their makeshift bunkers in time.

Many of the Vietnamese had built crude bunkers next to their hooches. The bunker's protection was not sophisticated, just mud mixed with straw overlaying some simple wood beams that could shelter three or four family members. A direct hit on the bunker would certainly kill the occupants, but it could easily withstand the shrapnel from a nearby explosion. Unfortunately the sudden barrage of mortars gave little warning and many had been caught in the open doing their daily chores.

The smoke was clearing as we entered the vill. Not a shot was fired. Any VC who might have been in the vill would have bugged out at the first explosion. They knew heavy fire meant we had a plan and would be moving on them. Some of the thatched roof structures leaned to one side from the blasts cutting their support poles. Nothing was burning. I looked at the vacant pit where the water buffalo we had killed resided just a few months ago. The small fence surrounding the pit was restored. I hoped a replacement buffalo was out working in the rice paddy.

Mortars had a low incendiary capability, but they created very high fragmentation. Upon entering the vill we encountered two Mama Sans carrying wounded children. The Mama Sans cried and screamed in Vietnamese, which we could not understand, but we understood their anger and frustration as they carried their bloody children. Two old men approached us limping with shrapnel wounds. Small streams of blood flowed down their legs onto the ground. Their wounds did not appear to be life-threatening and my mind flashed back to the indoctrination we had before entering Vietnam – "Don't respond with greater fire than you are taking!" Frankly, I did not buy into that notion. If I'm taking fire, I'm going to throw everything I have back. My thought was, "Some son-of-a-bitch is trying to kill me and I'm supposed to just trade bullets with him? Hell no!" The difference here was that we did not take a single bullet. I don't recall any deaths, thank God. Then competing emotions filled me. I felt sorry for the villagers, and at the same time I was angry that Riner did not accept my recommendation to avoid prepping the vill.

Riner walked into the vill shortly after me. I could tell from the look on his face he could not believe the result of what he had ordered. I'm sure his mind was saying to himself, "This can't be; I followed protocol!" I said nothing to him. I'm sure he could read my thoughts through a condescending stare, "You stupid asshole. Next time listen to our advice!" To his credit he called in an emergency priority one medevac chopper to take the wounded villagers to medical aid. Once the chopper arrived, we assisted loading the wounded and then moved on to set up for the night.

For the next two or three weeks we worked the area assigned to us. Surprisingly we had no major encounters with the VC or NVA. Riner seemed withdrawn, but more receptive to taking advice from his platoon commanders. Then we returned to Liberty Bridge for a week of recuperation. Our assignment was to protect the north side of the Bridge. The perimeter was small compared to the south side that housed Battalion Headquarters. Four-foot high berms surrounded the perimeter with two rows of concertina wire on top of them. Concertina wire was nasty stuff. It was not like conventional barbed wire with a single barb protruding from the wire. Concertina had razor sharp blades every six inches that could shred clothing and cut long gashes in the skin.

In the center of the perimeter were two bunkers fortified with logs and sandbags. To enter the bunker one had to duck low and take a couple of steps down. Inside, on the dirt floor, stood four cots. We used our own ponchos for bedding and cover. This was considered the officers' and non-commissioned officers' quarters.

The mess hall was on the south side of the Bridge. To walk the half mile from the north side for a hot meal was not an inconvenience. It was also possible to bring back a couple of beers and relax in our bunker. After dinner we returned to the north side and prepared to hit the rack. Riner, my platoon sergeant and I relaxed while sitting on our cots and enjoying our second beer. We began to loosen up and the conversation became casual as we shared some of our background and stories from home. Riner had only been our commanding officer for about a month. Although he had not earned my respect, I was beginning to recognize the stress he was feeling. I think a couple of beers allowed him to open up and share a more personal side. We finished our beer and prepared to go to sleep. Riner pulled out his .45 pistol to empty it. Like all of us, he carried his pistol with a round in the chamber and the hammer half-cocked. A half-cocked pistol was actually the safest position when a round was in the chamber. The trigger will not activate the hammer and if it is dropped, the hammer will not slam the firing pin on to the bullet. I never unloaded my pistol. I felt it was safe enough in the half-cocked position and I never knew when I would be scrambling to get hold of it. I did not want to think about using two hands to pull the slide and load a bullet. Just use my thumb to pull back the hammer and I was ready to fire.

While holding his pistol in his right hand, Riner placed his left hand on the barrel to pull the slide back and eject the bullet out of the chamber. His palm was about to grab the slide when his pistol went off! He dropped the pistol and pulled his left hand to his chest, grasping it with his good hand. His eyes appeared like headlights and he was unable to speak. The sergeant and I almost fell off our cots at the blast of the pistol. No one expects a shot to be fired while you are sitting around enjoying a beer!

Now Riner's pistol was lying on the floor, fully loaded, cocked and ready to fire. My sergeant picked up the pistol, reset the half-cock safety and laid it on one of the cots. I scrambled out of the bunker and yelled for Doc. Riner's palm had what appeared to be a small round hole, no more than a quarter inch in diameter. I would have expected a larger hole from a 45 caliber pistol, but on reflection I now know the size of the bullet does not always result in the size of the wound. Flesh tends to collapse around the wound, making it look smaller. The bullet had exited the side of Riner's left hand. This was not a round hole, to my surprise, but rather a slice like someone took a pocket knife and stuck it in the side of his hand. Doc arrived and bandaged Riner's wound. Then Riner walked to the south side of the Bridge where there was a small aid station. We never saw him again, and I will always wonder if this was an accident or a self-inflicted wound resulting from a melancholy moment of reflection. Maybe after a couple of beers he lost his concern for safety and just fumbled while ejecting that bullet. I didn't know, nor did I care. I hoped our next commander would have his shit together!

Although Riner's wound was not that serious, I'm sure Battalion command recognized the difficulty of returning him to command our company. What kind of trust and confidence would his troops have after their commander had put a bullet through his own hand?

sixteen

AN OLD-FASHIONED TRENCH WAR

Six miles southeast of Liberty Bridge was a low mountain range. Having grown up in Colorado it didn't qualify as a mountain range to me, but rather as a ridge of foothills that rose above the delta four to five hundred feet. The ridge was densely forested jungle which provided abundant watershed for the rice paddies on the delta between it and the Song Thu Bon River. It also provided a great hiding place for the Viet Cong and their caches of weapons, food and clothing.

We had started working an area near the base of the ridge line heading west toward the regimental post at An Hoa. We approached a small river flowing from the foothills into the delta and northward to the Song Thu Bon River. My map showed this river as the Cay Khe Vinh Trinh, named after the reservoir from which it flowed in the foothills. The terrain was not suitable for villages or rice paddies as the gentle rise and fall of the ground did not lend itself to growing rice. The foliage confined our movement to defined trails. It was not thick jungle reaching high over our heads, but rather heavy brush eight to ten feet high. It would be thick for 50 yards and then opened up into small grassy meadows. That pattern of thick, open, thick, open continued as we approached the small river making it difficult to pinpoint our exact location.

Our concern for booby traps escalated. A favorite placement of booby traps was where movement channeled us through an opening in the brush, or on a well-defined trail where the steep terrain forced us onto that trail. We surveyed the ground meticulously before each step, looking for a thin wire, a small depression, rises on the trail, or a piece of wood or a branch that simply looked out of place. While in single file, every man tried to step exactly where the man in front of him had stepped.

As we broke through the last brush thicket, the small river appeared less than a hundred yards in front of us. It was fairly shallow and slow moving, chest deep at most and no more than thirty yards wide. The opposite shore line was visible for a couple hundred yards to our left and the bank fell off sharply to the water. I noticed a couple of bomb craters in the opening between us and the river. The size of the craters surprised me, at least eight feet deep and fifteen to twenty feet across. These craters could not have been made from 500 pounder bombs normally used for close air support. A much larger explosive had created them. They could have been made from 2000 pounders dropped from B-52s conducting "Arc Light" missions, but that did not make sense either because only thirty yards separated these two craters. Bomb craters from B-52s are usually farther apart. The only other possibility could be shelling from 16 inch guns from the battleships off the coast. The coast was about twelve miles away and 16 inch guns could easily shoot a 2200 pound projectile over 25 miles. We had heard the roaring sound of these large shells pass over us on other occasions.

As we walked toward the craters in the open, we did not maintain single file and everyone spread out as we approached the river. Suddenly there was a loud explosion fifty yards on our right flank. The magnitude of the blast was greater than a hand grenade. I had no idea what it was, possibly an RPG (Rocket Propelled Grenade), maybe a booby trap. Simultaneously with the explosion came a swarm of automatic rifle fire from the other side of the river. The firing was a mix of rifle and heavy machine guns. Tracers came hot and heavy all around us. Most of the platoon was still behind me in the thick brush with only about a dozen of us in the open. We dove into the craters for cover. Everyone was peeking over the berm of his crater, firing their M-16s on full automatic and changing clips as fast as possible. Within a few seconds someone yelled, "Doc, Doc!" I could see a Marine waving his arm next to a body in a low spot near where the blast occurred. I feared the worst for the motionless body.

There was no way we could move on the enemy. Crossing the river in the open would have been certain suicide. The gooks knew we could not move on them and they dug in to fight. They would keep us pinned down in these craters and throw as much lead at us as possible until they saw the first artillery burst or a jet overhead. Then they would "get the hell out of Dodge." They could see us, but we could not see them. They had concealed themselves in the thick brush on the other side of the river. All we could do was try to spot the source of the tracers and return fire at that location.

I needed to get artillery or air support ASAP. I already had my map out. I could see the ridge line and the small river on the map. I knew our approximate location within a few hundred yards, but I had to know our exact location to call in artillery. I could not see any prominent terrain features, like a village or hill top, to get a compass reading. All I could do was give the Fire Control Center our general location, but it would have to be air support, not artillery support. Since the firing was coming from the other side of the river, I had a reasonable fix on the gooks' location, but I needed to know how far down the river from us they were shooting. I propped up on my elbows and peered over the edge of the berm. I don't think my head was above the berm more than three seconds. All I saw was a bunch of little green dots vibrating in front of me (they used green tracers). It looked like someone holding a laser light with a nervous hand.

It was tracers coming right at me! I ducked down and rolled over on my back as the berm of the crater took the impact of the machine gun fire. The dirt flew over the rim of the berm on me and a spent tracer bullet landed on my chest. I couldn't believe it; "that bullet had my name on it!" I picked it off my chest. The bullet was blistering hot. I quickly put it in my pocket. Why? I don't know; it just seemed the right thing to do at the time. My short visual over the berm gave me a reasonable idea of the location of the gooks. I told my radioman, "I think I have their location." He handed me the radio handset and I called Battalion Fire Control to explain our situation. Upon reflection, I wonder if Battalion Fire Control was trained in reading the urgency of voices calling for support, or if they heard the chaos of shooting and explosions taking place over the radio. Whatever it was, it didn't matter. Their response was fantastic. After giving them our approximate location and the location of the fire coming from the gooks, there was a pause. Then a voice came back, "We have an OV-10 on station that can respond in 3 minutes." (OV-10 is a quiet aircraft, twin turbo prop engines and able to carry a good amount of firepower: rockets and 20mm machine guns.) The exchange of fire continued, and I hoped we would not take more casualties.

The OV-10 came in low on the gooks' side of the river. I'm sure the pilot could confirm his target from the green tracers being fired at us. The OV-10's first pass was rockets and that was all that was needed. The firing stopped. The gooks knew there was no use in keeping up the fight. I looked to my right and saw Doc working on the lifeless Marine. I looked across the river and saw nothing but brush and water. There was no way to see if any of the enemy had given up their lives. Fortunately we took only one casualty. This encounter highlighted a typical frustration: no sense of victory or success, just survival, for the rest of us.

seventeen

MONSOON HERO

We had been on patrol for three weeks in the delta south of the Bridge. The monsoon rains had descended upon us and encounters with the gooks had became very light, just an occasional burst of fire from a remote tree line and then they would bug out after emptying a clip at us. I don't think they liked the rainy season any more than we did. For us the monsoon made it difficult to fight. It was impossible to call in air support because of the low-hanging clouds, and getting a medevac was often delayed until a break in the weather developed. It was difficult to recognize terrain features that gave us accurate coordinates for calling in artillery. The risk of giving wrong coordinates and having artillery land on us or a friendly vill was too high. The clouds enveloped us and formed a thick blanket at treetop level. The drizzle was relentless and made it impossible to stay dry. Although the temperature was in the mid to low 60's, having our clothing soaked made it feel like hypothermia was draining our strength constantly. Being active by walking during a patrol seemed to help, but once we stopped or set in for the night we would shake with chills.

I was concerned about having to call in a medevac if any of my men got sick from hypothermia or trench foot. In an effort to prevent anyone from getting trench foot I called for frequent breaks and ordered the men to remove their boots and socks. The soles of our feet would turn white and pucker up like prunes. It was imperative that we let our feet get some fresh air and wring out the water in our socks as best we could. Sometimes the skin would roll off the bottoms of our feet and expose raw flesh as if a huge blister had been removed, yet it did not hurt. The sponginess of our soaked socks and boots seemed to cushion the tenderness of our feet and the cold kept them numb. Trench foot could be so serious that it could result in the loss of toes. I was determined to avoid medevacs for trench foot in this weather. The monsoon season was one of the most miserable times to be in the bush.

We had been in the bush for a month, and we were overdue to rotate for a week at Battalion Headquarters. Thankfully we got the call to report to the Bridge so we headed for the dirt road that ran north from An Hoa. We were less than a couple hundred yards from the road when one of the men behind me, Ericson, hit a booby trap. The familiar call, "Doc, Doc!" rang out and I ran back to where Ericson was down on his back. Doc beat me to him and was already surveying the damage. Ericson was motionless. His wide-open eyes showed that distant stare of amazement like he was in a trance. He said nothing and was moving deeper into shock. Doc injected a shot of morphine and started to bandage multiple shrapnel wounds on Ericson's left side. Then Doc turned to me and said, "He is definitely a priority one!"

While I went back to get on the radio for calling in the medevac, four other men placed Ericson on a poncho and carried him up to the road. The radio was already on the open network for our area and I called, "This is Delta-1 Actual. We have a priority one medevac." Then I gave the coordinates of our location and told Air Control we had arrived at the road between Liberty Bridge and An Hoa. The response was disheartening, "Delta-1, we do not have a chopper in your area that can respond given the weather conditions." Before I could ask when a chopper would be available, a voice interrupted and said, "Delta-1 we are less than five minutes from your location and can pick up your wounded." I was confused that Marine Air Control had just said nothing was available and now I had someone willing to come through the low clouds and pick up our wounded... amazing! Air Control must have had misinformation, but I did not care as long as someone was willing to come through this soup to pick up Ericson.

I began communicating directly with the chopper pilot who was willing to come in to our location. I did not recognize his call sign, but assured him we were not in a "hot zone" (not taking enemy fire) and located on a well-defined road. Soon we could hear the sound of the chopper's rotor blades as it gently lowered itself through the thick layer of clouds at tree top level. The chopper appeared about a quarter mile away just above the road. We popped a yellow smoke canister to identify our position and pitched it in the center of the road. The chopper hovered above the road, pivoted left and then right in an effort to locate us. It was evident the moment they saw the yellow smoke. It reminded me of a hunting dog seeing its objective and running to retrieve it. The chopper's tail lifted up and the nose dropped so the main rotor could propel it forward. The rotor blades appeared as if they could be hitting the road as it sped toward us. The chopper couldn't have been more than fifteen feet off the road bed when I could see a swirling cloud of misty water and red mud flying off the road behind it. Just as it got to the yellow smoke canister its nose flared up and the skids gently settled on the road. It was a 101st Air Cavalry Huey Gun Ship. Now I understood why Marine Air Control did not know about the Army chopper.

The machine gunners stood in the open side doors of the gunship. Four men quickly loaded Ericson onto the floor of the chopper. I walked up to the pilot's window. I knocked on the window to thank the pilot. He turned to me and gave me a thumbs-up. As I looked into his face my thought was, "This kid can't be more than twenty at the most." The insignia on his collar was that of a Warrant Officer, one grade below Lieutenant. This was a young Army pilot who must have made it through the flight program and earned his wings as a Warrant Officer! Upon reflection, I can appreciate the gutsy nature of that young pilot. At that age it was easy to feel invincible. And commanding a million-dollar piece of equipment with twin machine guns and rockets allowed for the confidence to take the risk.

I'm thankful for the guts that young pilot displayed that day. I will forever have the highest regard and respect for the Army's 101st Air Cavalry!

Sitting on the edge of a bomb crater
in a rain jacket trying to endure the monsoon season.
Notice the low poncho-tent behind me.

eighteen

THE ARIZONA

The reputation of the Arizona Territory was well known to every Marine located south of Da Nang. Even Division Headquarters in Da Nang was aware of the hard fighting that routinely took place in the Arizona. There was good reason this area was given the title of the "Arizona." Foremost was the fierce fighting that reminded us of the badlands of Arizona, home to thieves and gunslingers back in the 1800s. It seemed the VC and NVA fought like crazy men and didn't give a damn if they got killed. Then there was the desolate terrain. It was flat and barren with far fewer rice paddies than the lush delta on the other side of the river, which made movement out of the mountains easy for the enemy. Under cover of night they could carry their rockets within range of An Hoa in just a few hours. Virtually all of the rockets fired on Regimental Headquarters at An Hoa came from the Arizona.

Operations to sweep the Arizona seemed to occur with regularity. When the sweeps started, the initial fire fights would be intense as the gooks fled to the mountain range bordering the southwest edge of the Arizona. They would disappear into the mountains just like ants into a mound of sand. Then the gooks would move back into the Arizona within a day or two after having been pushed out by a couple of companies. It was a never-ending cycle and our turn was sure to come up.

The monsoon rains had stopped, and it was blistering hot when our company got the call to participate in a sweep of the Arizona. Since there was no bridge over the river from An Hoa, that left only two ways to get there, by boat or helicopter. Crossing the river by boat was slow, exposed us too much and gave the enemy lots of warning that a sweep was in progress. Helicopters flew out of An Hoa constantly. Everyone within a five mile radius, even the enemy, was numb to the frequency of flights in and out of the base. A sudden change of course to cross the river into the Arizona would take only ten minutes and increased the element of surprise.

The operation was planned to take only a couple of days and we expected to be resupplied within twenty-four hours; loading up with lots of provisions was not necessary. After filling our canteens, most of us put only one or two C-rations in our packs. We would be moving fast and covering a lot of ground, so keeping the weight down was essential. It was more important to carry extra ammo than chow.

The spinning twin rotors of the CH-46 helicopter fanned us with a refreshing wind as we walked up the rear loading ramp and took our places on the canvas seats hanging from each side of the chopper. Two CH-46's had the capacity needed to ferry my platoon to the other side of the river. Two Huey gunships would escort us into the landing zone. Once the landing zone was identified, the Hueys would make low passes on the tree lines bordering the landing zone. If we took any fire while landing, the Hueys would respond with rockets and machine gun fire.

Landing in an unknown location and not knowing what to expect is one of the most frightening experiences of combat. It was like being packed in like sardines in this capsule hovering above the ground, knowing that one burst from a machine gun could kill most, if not all of us. I now know what those soldiers must have felt as they landed on the beaches of Normandy. No one talked as we boarded the choppers. Although the webbed canvas seats faced each other, everyone seemed to avoid eye contact. Each man seemed consumed in his own thoughts. I'm sure some fell deep into prayer mode. I did not try to initiate conversation, but rather let each man reconcile the moment in his own way. I also was scared and felt that knot in my gut as I worried, "What if the landing zone is hot with enemy fire while we are crowded on this chopper and unable to respond? Man! What a bunch of sitting ducks!"

The loading ramp on the back of the chopper lifted up and the sound of the rotors intensified. Soon we ascended to 3,000 feet, just enough altitude to minimize the effect of small arms fire from the ground. The river was visible from the opening above the loading ramp. As soon as we crossed the river we started our descent. It seemed like the flight took less than a minute. The ramp started to drop before the chopper settled on the ground. I don't think the wheels had touched the ground when six men preceded me off the chopper. I never saw a chopper evacuation that fast in all my training… ten seconds, maybe fifteen at most. Everyone cleared the chopper by about twenty yards and formed a crescent perimeter while lying prone with all weapons pointed toward the nearest tree line. The Huey gunships roared overhead still making their low-level passes over the tree line, ready to fire at a moment's notice if we encountered any resistance. Fortunately, not a shot was fired and we moved quickly into the cover of the trees.

After collecting ourselves, we started our movement through the Arizona. We headed north, with Charlie Company on our left flank, between us and the mountain range. We protected the right flank of the operation. This was fine with me. The farther from that mountain range, where the worst fighting took place, the better. The villages seemed like ghost towns, as if everyone had abandoned their homes. The abandonment made sense, the more I thought about it. This territory was heavily occupied by the VC and NVA. It was certain that reprisals would be taken against any villagers that aided us, so the village people got out of the way and avoided any contact with us when a sweep was being conducted.

We set up the first night in a small vill that was vacant. The next day we continued our march and again there was no contact with the enemy. Charlie Company had some brief skirmishes on our left flank, but not a major fight. The sweep was in its second day. It was clear that all the VC and NVA knew what was happening. They had bugged out.

We expected resupply the morning of the second day, but due to heavy fighting elsewhere all choppers had to support other units. We did not need more ammunition, but the lack of food was beginning to wear on everyone. It was the end of our second day and most of us had eaten only one C-ration. The continuous walking and sweating without food was starting to feel like a death march. All I had left was a roll of Life Savers in my pocket. I remember eating two or three for breakfast and the same for lunch. I was desperately trying to make them last as long as possible. Lack of water was not a problem. Each village had a well or access to water nearby.

At the end of the second day we set up in another abandoned vill and found a cultivated patch of peanuts. It was like finding a treasure. Everyone dug up what they wanted and roasted them in the metal cups that fit on the bottom of our canteens. I harvested, shelled and roasted about five handfuls. They tasted fantastic! Later that night, as the sun was setting, I walked the perimeter to check on where the men had set up. In one position three men had gathered under a poncho that was propped up to form a low tent. I heard them chatting in what sounded like joyful conversation. As I peered around the corner of the poncho-tent there sat three Marines gathered around a helmet propped up with sticks containing boiling water and a plucked chicken! My sudden presence shocked them. Their faces took on a look of fear mixed with guilt as if a kid had been caught with his hand in the cookie jar. On the contrary, I was

Air strike in the Arizona between us and the mountain range.
Charlie Company must have called it in.

Chowing down on the peanuts I found
and roasted while in an abandoned village.

impressed with their ingenuity and resourcefulness. The helmet, with its liner removed, was a perfect kettle for their purpose. There was no fire and I could tell they had no C-4 to heat the water so I asked, "What are you guys using to boil it?" With a sheepish response one of the Marines said, "Hand grenades!" "Hand grenades?" I exclaimed. I was amazed and could not believe it was possible to heat with a hand grenade. They had unscrewed and removed the top of the grenade that held the pin, safety-lever and blast-cap. Then, using a knife, they pried out the metal liner that held the blast-cap, exposing the explosive in the grenade. Then they ignited the explosive. The principle was the same as lighting a ball of C-4, but the grenade produced an intense blue-orange flame that shot up eighteen inches from the top of the grenade. The flame lasted for a couple of minutes and sounded like a blow-torch turned up full blast. The flame enveloped the helmet. After two grenades the water was steaming. I'm not sure how many grenades it took to cook that chicken. I would guess three to four depending on how hungry they were. Regardless, I was impressed and did not reprimand them for using a weapon to make their dinner. In fact, I congratulated them.

On the third day we completed our sweep and the CH-46 choppers picked us up that afternoon to take us back to An Hoa. We ended our effort as uneventfully as it started. Not a shot was fired. Thankfully the Arizona did not live up to its reputation for us. Although we did have to replenish some hand grenades. Fire fights are no fun and anyone wishing to get in one should see a psychiatrist.

RECIPE FOR BUSH BOILED CHICKEN

- *One helmet without liner*
- *One scrawny plucked whole chicken*
- *Water to cover bird*
- *4-5 hand grenades*
- *Prop helmet 12 to 18 inches off ground with sticks or rocks*
- *Place chicken and water in helmet*
- *Remove blast-cap and blast well from hand grenades*
- *Ignite hand grenade and place under helmet. Use two grenades initially to bring to boil. Ignite one grenade every 10 minutes until chicken is tender.*

nineteen

FROM BUSH TO R&R TO BUSH

Platoon commanders had a high casualty rate after six to eight months in the bush. What contributed to the casualty rate was overconfidence. Platoon commanders, including me, gained a high comfort level with their men's capabilities, as well as our own, over time. We also developed an awareness and appreciation of the tactics of the enemy. This grew to a point where overconfidence began to creep into our judgment. I call this the "John Wayne" syndrome. My self-assurance, as well as my fellow platoon commanders', grew to a point where we became overly optimistic that we could succeed in any situation. We would take risks that never entered our minds in the first few months of commanding our platoons. On one occasion I got feedback from some of my men that I was taking too many chances. This overconfidence by platoon commanders was recognized by higher command. As a result it was common practice to rotate platoon commanders out of the bush into support roles at Battalion or Regimental bases after eight months.

Dear Diana,

I'm not to sure about what is going on, but today a new 2/Lt came into our company and he is Taking over my platoon! Sounds like its out of The bush for me! EH? His name is Pilkington and he graduated from basic school in November and went to HILT, that is why he is just getting over here. But that is OK with me just as long as he is here. Tomorrow we are going to run a patrol together and then he will mostlikely take it over Lock-stock & Barrel. Yahoooo! And in 17 days I'll be seeing you in Hawaii for a hell of a good Time. OK? About 3 hrs. Later and I'm just nervous as all get out because I don't No what They have in store for me. Wish They would be more concret as to what I'm going to be doing. Time will go so much more slowly now, since I haven't got a platoon of my own. I guess I'll just join The CP and remain There untill I leave for R & R.

FEBRUARY 11, 1969 | LIBERTY BRIDGE | TYPESET PAGE 231

I had more bush time than any other platoon commander in the battalion and was feeling confident I would be next for rotation to a rear position. Out of the blue I got word I was being replaced by a lieutenant named Pilkington. Although this was his first tour in Nam and he was "green," I took a liking to him right off the bat. His nickname was Chip. He was short, but stood tall with confidence. Upon reflection I would say he reminded me of Audie Murphy[1], the most decorated soldier of WWII. Chip was unassuming and eager to learn about the platoon and how they performed in the bush. I could see he was motivated to lead. We worked a couple of patrols together and I gave him as much information as possible regarding the skills, abilities, and character of the men in the platoon. Then I turned my platoon over to Chip and caught the next resupply chopper back to An Hoa, Regimental Headquarters, where I would assume the duties of Headquarters and Support Executive Officer for the battalion. I would spend two weeks in An Hoa before traveling to Hawaii to meet Diana for R&R (Rest & Relaxation).

Those five days with Diana were a wonderful break from the dirt, sweat and grime of the war. We enjoyed our time together relaxing on the beach and eating wonderful food in restaurants. It was like a dream. On the last two days of our reunion my guts started to twirl like a roller coaster. One minute I was fine. The next minute I had to find a restroom or I was certain to crap my pants. Little did I know what plagued me until I returned to Vietnam.

The return to An Hoa rekindled the same anxiety I had when I first landed there six months earlier. This time the anxiety focused on what expectations would be of me as Executive Officer of Headquarters & Support. I soon learned my new job would have to wait. Delta Company had lost their commander of the 3rd platoon. Yup, I was now "Delta-3 Actual." I would much rather have rejoined my old platoon (Delta-1). I knew the men in Delta-1 and they knew me. I understood their capabilities and whom to trust in difficult situations. However, my replacement, Lt. Pilkington, was doing a good job.

Dearest Diana,   Mar. 10.
                                        1315

          I just finished a patrol This
morning down past phu Lôc (2). Right
now we are on a hill just off a road near
my Lôc (2) about 913 513. Boy! have I got
a bad attitude now that I'm back in the
bush. And I'm twice as ~~sure~~ worried as
ever! I'm sure it is because of the outstanding
time we had on R&R. I didn't believe I
was in such bad shape until that patrol
to day when I was walking along and sweating
like crazy. Plus my Trousers don't fit
either. Boy! did I get spoiled. But
it was fun. I can't believe it was over
so fast. Will I ever be glad to get back
to the rear where I can at least ~~feel~~ feel
clean once in a while. I can't find anything
to say I'm in such a shitty mood. I
shouldn't even be writting a letter because
it probably depresses you also. No sooner
had I gotten back to the bush and I could
roll the dirt off me.

Now I am the Third platoon Comdr. They are not as good as the "Fighting First" but better than some I have seen. The big thing is I don't know how long I'm going to be here. Surelly (sp) not more than a month I hope!?!?! Things are drying up and it is getting hotter. I'm cooking, I can't even imagine what summer will be like. Why is it I miss you so much just after having been with you not more than a week ago. But I feel worse than when I first left. Wish I would get a letter from you. Should be pretty soon. If you wrote the day I left, but I'm sure you were too busy. How is Kona? nice and out of the way? Wish I was there but may as well wish for the moon! I'm in a crudy mood so I'll close for now may-be I feel better Tomorrow. Thanks for such a wonderful time in Hawaii. I'll never forget it as long as we live. Be a good kid and put on some pounds (in the right places) I love you so much it hurts.

Frank.

MARCH 10, 1969 | IN THE BUSH | TYPESET PAGE 232

135

The TET offensive was just starting to fire up. TET was Vietnam's celebration of "the lunar new year," the arrival of spring. The 1968 TET offensive had been very bloody and intelligence was saying that this year could be just as bad. For some reason this holiday inspired the gooks to go crazy and fight like madmen. We made frequent patrols through vills looking for weapons and men of fighting age. Each patrol yielded nothing. We took no sniper fire, walking through a vill was like walking through a morgue. Strangely, it was like the VC had gone underground.

Dearest Diana,   15th March.
                                   21:22
    I'm on the other side of the bridge and this is the side where people hang a little bit more Loosly. And do a little too much drinking. I'm havent touched a drop since R&R! Just finised "The Pres.'s Plane is missing." Not too bad! I'm surprised it held my intrest. Recieved your letter of the 8th. Your new Job sounds Nice. Meet quite a few people. You said the people are so nice and casual. Just make sure you don't get tooooo casual with the

natives! The "deli" sound great!
I haven't lost any wt. yet. I
have actually only been in the bush
for 3 days and it has been quite
like I have never seen. I think
all their man power is centered
around the bigger instclations
during this offensive. I've given
up my frustration about not knowing
my emidiate destiny, And reclined to
the fact that I'm in the bush and
I'll stay here until (?) I just polyreed
my-self out to the facts. Your letters
sound so cheery. I'm sure happy
you seem so much more at ~~any~~
ease or something now. Like
a flower budding or something
reincarnating. there is a world of
difference in your letters. You
can't tell, but I sure ~~can~~. I think
you will injoy your job, etc. ; put

OK. some a't. But not too much

OK. Not over 130lb. OK? One thing

I regret about your job is you won't

be able to write so often on the

job, as you did at The bank.

but may-be the goodies will

surfice.

MARCH 15, 1969 | LIBERTY BRIDGE | TYPESET PAGE 233

1. Audie Murphy: Became the most decorated United States soldier of World War II during twenty-seven months in action in the European Theatre. (Wikipedia)

 DIANA'S REFLECTION PAGE 209

twenty

BATTLE AT LIBERTY BRIDGE

Everyone referred to Liberty Bridge as "the Bridge." It was located twelve miles south of Da Nang and ten miles north of An Hoa. Spanning the Song Thu Bon River, it provided a major supply route from Da Nang to the 5th Marine Regiment in An Hoa. This was crucial for supporting combat units in the bush. The road from Da Nang to An Hoa was called Liberty Road, hence the name for the Bridge.

The Seabees (Naval Construction) are to be complimented for the stoutness of their construction. It was the longest wooden bridge in Vietnam (over 2000 feet long). Although the bridge had only one lane, it easily supported tanks and large troop transports. Flags could be raised at both ends of the bridge to signal which direction was safe for travel. The Seabees constructed a small hill on the south side of the bridge. This was the headquarters of the 1st Battalion, 5th Marine Regiment. The hill gave them a good field of view around their perimeter. Tents and bunkers covered that hill. Pits for artillery and mortars ringed the perimeter behind multiple rows of concertina wire. Two tanks resided in the compound. They escorted convoys from the bridge south to An Hoa. I felt this much firepower and protection was a bit of overkill. We had nothing on the north side to compare to the south side's defenses, just machine guns, LAAWs and a couple of 60mm mortars. The rationale was that the south side could respond adequately if the north side was attacked.

As TET approached, the Battalion commander pulled Delta and Charlie companies into Liberty Bridge for added security. My old platoon (Delta-1) was on the south side of the bridge manning the lines around the Battalion Headquarters. My new platoon (Delta-3) and I manned the positions on the north side. It was a much smaller perimeter and not elevated on a hill like the south side. Since the terrain was flat, we could see for at least two hundred yards in front of our perimeter. This gave us a good field of fire for anything approaching our position.

Going north from the bridge to Da Nang was fairly safe, but going south along the eastern border of the Arizona could get hairy with road mines, booby traps and occasional sniper fire. The tanks helped greatly in escorting the convoys traveling from the Bridge to An Hoa.

The north and south perimeters of the bridge consisted of tent camps encircled with dirt berms four feet high, and two rows of concertina wire on top of the berms. The perimeter had bunkers every forty to fifty yards, which were manned by two or three men with machine guns.

We could get some beer at the Bridge, but my guts were still killing me since returning from R&R. Everything was running through me like water. I was weak and in a bad mood.

Things seemed really quiet while on patrol and nothing was happening; there were no encounters of any kind, not even the occasional sniper fire from a tree line. It was eerie and worrisome how calm the bush had become. We passed the time just sitting around at the Bridge. Headquarters at the Bridge was much better than the bush. The hot meals and showers really helped, but the boredom settled in after a few days.

We had been at the Bridge for three days. Sometime after midnight the sounds of explosions woke me. I grabbed my helmet and flak vest and ran out of the bunker. It was like daylight outside with all the illumination flares in the sky. I ran to the berm surrounding our perimeter. The firing was intense with tracers and bullets flying everywhere. Every man was positioned on the perimeter trading rifle and machine gun fire coming from the tree line hundreds of yards away. The battle on the other side of the bridge was intense. The sky was lit up like the 4th of July with illumination flares floating from their small parachutes. I could see tracers coming off their perimeter in every direction as the explosions came in a constant roar. We started receiving some explosions inside our perimeter. They could not have been heavy artillery or rockets. They must have been RPG's or mortars. I hated taking mortar fire. I could hear that thumping sound from the mortars being fired a quarter mile away, knowing they would soon come in on us. It is a strange feeling when you are in a fight like this. There is no time to be scared. You rely on your training and bush experience and try to keep your wits about you. Time seems to float in suspended animation. That twenty to thirty seconds it took the mortars to come in on us after hearing them being fired was like going to the dentist. You knew it was going to hurt. All you wanted was to get it over with as soon as possible.

We continued to trade small arms fire for a couple of hours while the south side of the bridge was getting pounded. There was no way we could call in artillery or mortars from the 105mm howitzers or 81mm mortars on the south side. They had to focus on fighting their own battle. As I listened on the radio it was total chaos. I think I responded only once or twice to inquiries about our status. I can't remember what I said, but I'm sure it was something close to, "Holding our own!" My adrenalin was pumping. I felt useless. All I could do was encourage everyone to return as much fire as possible. Giving commands during a fire fight is next to impossible. No one can hear you over the shooting and the explosions. My men's performance was fantastic. They knew what to do. They pulled extra ammo out of the ammo bunker and made sure the machine guns had plenty of firepower. My respect for the men in the 3rd platoon grew greatly as I went from bunker to bunker giving encouragement.

The gooks' strategy was well conceived; engage both ends of the bridge so neither side could help the other. Then focus on the south side where the Battalion Headquarters and heavy equipment was located. They wanted to destroy the ammunition dumps, tanks, and battalion leadership. They knew air support could not be called in if they got inside the perimeter. Their strategy worked. We could not get mortar or artillery support from the south side, and there was no possibility for some of us to move to the south side and help in their fight. It would have been crazy to cross a half mile long bridge in the open and weaken our position, which would have given the gooks an opportunity to overrun us and blow up the bridge from our side. No! We had to stick it out and hold off as best we could.

The assault stopped as abruptly as it had started. We remained in our positions on the berm, surveying the open ground in front of us as the illumination flares continued to burn overhead. It was quiet. Everyone remained vigilant, fearing a second wave, but it never came. Now the realization of what had happened started to set in. I could feel myself shaking, just like I did after other fire fights in the bush. I can only guess that the shakes came from an intense feeling of relief and the adrenalin starting to subside. The eastern sky started to glow purple-orange as a new day was coming upon us.[1]

Dearest Wife,   *Mar. 19*
                                                   1969

One year ago today I graduated & was commissioned! Time sure has gone by fast! I just hope it continues to pass by as fast. Last nite we took 5 or 6 incoming rockets that just missed the ammo dump. The other side of the bridge had a full fledged attack. They got inside the wire and started blowing bunkers and buildings. Fifteen were killed and 70 some gooks got it. I'm sure you will hear about it if you haven't already. Anyway they sure payed for it. They must have been doped up on drugs because it was sure a suicide mission. Some were found with hands and legs blown off and still fighting with turniquits on their stumps. It was a real blood bath, I'm glad I wasn't on that side of the bridge. I don't know when we will be going back to the bush, soon I hope. This stuff is getting old.

MARCH 19, 1969 | LIBERTY BRIDGE | TYPESET PAGE 233

Since my old platoon, Delta-1, was on the south side, I was concerned about how they came out of the fight. I walked across the bridge after the sun had been up for a couple of hours. There was an eerie somberness as I approached the south side. Everyone was cleaning up the carnage without conversation. As I walked up the road to the top of the hill where the command bunker was located, I followed the tread marks left by one of the tanks. Then I passed a gook that had been crushed by the tread of a tank. His body was missing from his rib-cage down. The only things visible were mangled arms and his head. I could see blood and guts ground into the dirt among the tread marks. As I looked around I could not believe the carnage. Some of the enemy bodies still lay caught in the concertina wire. All the dead Marines had been removed and covered, awaiting air lift to Da Nang. When I got to the top of the hill I encountered some of the men from my old platoon. They told me Doc had been killed. I could envision Doc running from one wounded Marine to another administering first aid, just as he had done in the bush. He would not have been engaged in the fight or looking for the enemy inside the compound. He was focused on his job–bringing aid and comfort to others.

I felt a deep sadness as I remembered how Doc cared for me when I was wounded, as well as the other Marines in the 1st platoon. Although I was upset about losing Doc, the sight of so many dead VC & NVA did not bother me. This was a victory I did not feel like celebrating. I will remember it forever. This was the ugliness of war and I had become immune to viewing the blood of the enemy - c'est la vie!

I checked in with the Battalion Command Post and let them know we had started to clean up the north side of the bridge and had taken only minor casualties. I learned that during the fight, the 106mm recoilless rifles on the south perimeter had fired flechette rounds at point blank range into the wire surrounding the compound. This was truly a last resort tactic. Each 106mm flechette round is filled with thousands of darts that can cover a football field with a deadly swath.

After seeing the result of the intense fight that took place at Battalion Headquarters and knowing the enemy had penetrated their defenses, I was thankful we were able to hold our position on the north side. Had the enemy attacked us with the same force, the outcome might have been very different.

1. The Battle of Liberty Bridge, early in the morning of March 19th, 1969 was one of the most significant battles fought by the 1st Marine Division in 1969. Fifteen Marines gave their lives when their position was overrun by a regimental force of NVA. Seventy-two of the enemy died in their attempt to destroy the command post of the 1st Battalion, 5th Marine Regiment.

twenty one

BULLETS MISSED BUT THE HOOK GOT ME

After having dealt with severe diarrhea since returning from R&R, it was time to get a medical opinion. So the next day after the battle at the Bridge I was sent to the Battalion medical station in Da Nang and was diagnosed with hookworm. Soon I learned that the hookworm has a life cycle in the human body that is very unpleasant. An infected person passes the eggs of a hookworm in their feces. While on the ground the egg develops into a tiny larva stage and then bores into our body through the pores of our feet. We frequently walked barefoot to dry our boots and air our feet. The larva migrates through the blood stream to the lungs and then matures to the next stage which is coughed up and swallowed. Finally, the mature larva enters the intestine and attaches, where it matures and starts the cycle over by excreting its eggs. I was issued a gelatin capsule the size of a marble that felt like swallowing a golf ball. The next day my anal orifice was lit up like a blowtorch. After a week of this treatment I finally started to feel normal. Fortunately, Diana never suffered from this unpleasant affliction even though our lips touched numerous times while on R&R.

Dear Diana, March 22

    Remember The trouble I was having 11:40 am.
with my guts on R&R? Well, it seemed to
be getting worse instead of better so I came in
to An HOA The 20th to have it looked into.
They took a sample of my "STOOL" (shit) and said
they found NOTHING but The "doc" asked ~~how~~ long
i have had The runs? ~~he~~ So when I said over
a month he sent me to 1st Medical Battalion in
Da Nang. There They took another stool sample, Blood
sample and stuck Tubes and pipes up my
ass!!! And it hurt. Well, They decided I
have Hook worms (from going bare foot), and Vasilary
Disentary. In other words The cronic shits with bugs.
They gave me 3 different types of medications (oral) to
take in sequence. One of The pills is suppose to
give me a real buzz. So I'm Not suppose to be
in The bush when I Take it. That means I'll probably
go to The bridge the 26th or 27th. Did you ~~know~~ hear
about The bridge? We were attacked The 18th I believe
and 72 gooks were Killed on The wire or inside The
wire surrounding The compound. I may have already
mentioned something about it. I can't remember so I'll
keep going. They had flame Throwers and, sachel
charges with an unbelievable amount of handgrenades.
Unfortunately 4 people from our unit died and 8 people
from The Artilery battery. Over 50 ~~people were~~ medivaced
out The ~~next~~ next day. And They had to dig a
hole with a bulldozer to burry all The dead gooks.
They VC & NVA payed a high price for what They accomplished.
It is amazing that so many got inside The barbed
wire surrounding that place! Right Now I'm in
An HOA and we have a New Captain To Take over

twenty two

A SMOKING LETTER

Within a week after the battle at Liberty Bridge I was relieved of my command of 3rd Platoon. I was assigned as Executive Officer of Headquarters & Support Company for the 1st Battalion, 5th Marine Regiment. My new job was located at Regimental Headquarters in An Hoa.

It had been about three weeks since I returned from meeting Diana in Hawaii for R&R. We had a wonderful time touring the island, relaxing on the beach and enjoying great dining, wine and shows. Diana had a long-time school friend, Sherry, who was living with two other women on the island of Hawaii in a small resort/fishing village named Kailua Kona. After R&R she planned to fly there and stay with her friend while I served out the rest of my tour in Nam. It sounded fine with me since it would be four girls sharing a house in a remote coastal town.

I did not particularly care for the administrative work my new job entailed. It included sitting in on court-martial hearings, administering payrolls as the Regimental Pay Master and coordinating supply deliveries. The routine of rockets hitting us on a daily basis was nerve-wracking. One of my main distractions was writing letters to Diana and getting letters from her. One day I received a letter from Diana that tipped me over the edge. She wrote about a person she befriended named "Stuart" and how they went to a movie together. She was clear in her letter to point out that Stuart considered his role as her protector and she wrote that it was a "big brother" relationship. During the first half of my tour Diana lived with her parents and worked as a teller in a bank. I found her letters comforting since I knew the territory and mutual friends we shared. Plus, living with her parents gave me a feeling of security for her. Our letters focused on mutual love for each other and encouragement that we could weather this difficult period in our lives. Maybe I read too much into this letter. Maybe our recent time together on R&R made me more homesick to be with her. Maybe I assumed there was too much freedom with her living with three bachelorettes in a coastal resort town. Whatever it was, my trust faltered and I retaliated. Here I was in a combat zone getting fired upon almost daily and my wife was going to a movie with another man! I was livid and fired off a letter that I'm sure singed the envelope:

Dear Diana,   April 4th.

I recieved your letter of the 30th
to day. Went to the movies last
night with Stuart. Cool! I'm
jealous. How do you expect
me to feel ~~ten~~ while you are
Dating some guy I don't know,
a thing about and I sit here
helpless. You must look pretty good
at 125 lbs. You always did. In
your letters you always say we
did this, meet the Gang, the Group,
or the Crowd. I'm sure you
are always next to Stuart,
or him next to you. I thought
his old girl friend was suppose
to go with him around the world.
How come all of sudden he stays
at Kona? And around you? You
are married and he doesn't or

149

should know better than to hang
around another man's wife! I'll
be coming to Kona some time between
now and July 31. You won't
know when, And I'm not going
to say. I think I'll just pop
in and when I do Tell Stuart
to stand by. Because if he is
with you And I don't care where or
what we are going to tangle. And
don't try to tell me his intentions
are good I don't believe it, I
never will. He is male you are
Female, figure it out! I can tell by
your letters your love for me is
waining. And you don't miss me anymore because you have someone else to
fill the gap. Now don't get me
wrong, Diana. I don't think you
are being unfaithful. But how

long will your will power hold out? I'll bet right now it is in The Big Brother Jope where you talk ~~talk~~ very seriously about your problems and worries. Most of which I'm sure concerns me. And he agrees, especially with your love for me and says how lucky a person I am to have a wife like you. I thought Those girls would provide you with enough companionship. A Kid just walked in with a letter for me from Mom. Says she is sick...oH Hell I'll just send it to you. Now Back to you and Stuart. I'm so damn jealous I have a sick feeling in my stomach and feel week all over. I didn't know I could even love you this much. But it is so strong and restrained I can't begine To

Tell you how I feel. Nothing to ~~tell~~ ~~it~~ release it on. Maybe if I go back to the bush it will take my mind off of it. Plus may-be I'll have something to vent my frustration on. I have no weapon against Stuart except the love you have or had for me. I have to rely on this and your good judgement. I had so much faith in you but it seems to be shaking a little. Most of all be Truthful in telling me what you are doing in your spare time. I want to know. But most of all I want you for the rest of my life. And as I said before I won't share any part of you any time, any where. Its all or NONE Diana.

Guess what! The Kid Just ~~become~~ come in with a package from you. It has a green chickie so I'll wore it in the rubber band around my helment for as long as it will ~~stay~~ stay in one piece or until some general tells me To take it off. And the ~~Easter~~ Easter basket is in A-1 shape. THANK You. You ~~an~~ Had 3 Black Russians! With who! ~~an~~ And on our anniversary. How would you feel if I went out and had
3 Drinks
~~them~~ with some girl, after I had Taken her to a movie. Don't go out with him anymore, Diana. I don't like it. And you don't need it. You haven't got problems so bad you Need a big brother. I don't trust him. I've got to catch a Helicopter out to Charlie Co. to pay them Their in the Horse Shoe.

Love Frank.

Now it is forty-three years later. As I read this letter I regret having ever written it. I failed to recognize one of the most fundamental foundations of love and marriage-trust. Diana and I are still together and enjoying our children and grandchildren.

However, as a word of advice, don't send a letter to a soldier in combat telling him or her that you enjoyed a movie with a member of the opposite sex while your spouse is in harm's way. It just doesn't ease the burden of war!

The Easter chick Diana sent me
in the band of my helmet.

 DIANA'S REFLECTION PAGE 210

twenty three

SHRAPNEL DOESN'T HURT

An Hoa was an expansive tent camp with a landing strip, which was a level dirt road that could accommodate C-130 cargo planes filled with troops and supplies. The performance of the C-130s impressed me greatly! They looked like a fat, short transport with two turbo props on each wing. They had a jet pack assist on both sides of the rear fuselage that would apply additional thrust to allow an extremely short take off with impressive gain in altitude. Gaining altitude was important to evade enemy ground fire once they cleared the runway. The rear drop ramp on a C-130 would allow loading and off-loading of light vehicles, jeeps and small armored vehicles.

Part of my responsibility as Executive Officer of Headquarters & Support Company was to interrogate and debrief prisoners captured in the field. A Kit Carson Scout was usually available to help with the interrogation process, but rarely did the interrogation reveal useful information. I suspect the realization that no harm would come to prisoners gave them confidence to withdraw and take a posture of ignorance or non-cooperation. As a result, they usually found themselves shipped off to Division Headquarters in Da Nang for a more in-depth interrogation.

My "hooch," where I slept, was a tent mounted on stilts. Raising the tents off the ground was necessary to allow the water from monsoon rains to flow freely through the camp without flooding the tents. The suspended floor was made of wooden planks. Three to four men could occupy each tent in relative comfort. We had cots to sleep on, but only our poncho covers for blankets, which was fine since most of the hot humid nights required no cover at all. There was a mess hall tent that served two hot meals each day-lunch and dinner. What a luxury!

Because our tents rested on a platform two to three feet in the air, there was a bunker of sandbags next to the steps leading outside the tent. The walls of the bunker stood about three feet high and it was open on top so we could dive into the bunker at a moment's notice. One of the worst places to be during an attack was in a tent elevated off the ground, because it gave much greater exposure to enemy rifle fire and also put us in the optimal shrapnel pattern for rockets and mortars. But it was better than sleeping in the mud and having the rain run through our hooch.

Helipads sat along the side of the runway where choppers could be loaded up for resupplying the troops in the field. Most resupply choppers were the twin rotor CH-46 by Boeing with one rotor in front and a second rotor in the rear. These twin rotors enabled the helicopter to lift a large cargo. CH-46 choppers delivered our supplies to the bush using suspended nets. The net would hang from the belly of the chopper. As it approached they would lower the net to the ground without landing and then release it to leave a pile of C-rations, mail and ammo. It was a resupply everyone welcomed!

Dearest Diana;   *16 May '69*
Right now I'm at the bridge and have spent the last ~~three~~ two nites and days here. Well, Babe, things don't look so good for the Kid! . . I believe they are going to make

Checking in a prisoner at Regimental Headquarters in An Hoa. Note the raised tents in the background.

CH-46 chopper delivering supplies to the field.

me Company Commander of His Co. and we will be going to the Arizona "bush." While we are discussing bad news, remember Lt. Pilkington, The Lt. That took over my plt? He was Killed two days ago, not over 1000 yds. from the bridge. That was a real bust! He was a damn fine Lt. and he was married to a very good looking woman. Fortunately, they had No children. What is the thing that makes the difference weather it is me or Pilkington? He was a good

friend and I feel a great loss now. Any Time someone I Know dies I feel a lose but this seems like such a waist. I'd better stop philosophizing or I'll really get down in the dumps.

MAY 16, 1969 | LIBERTY BRIDGE | TYPESET PAGE 236

I was devastated when I heard that Lt. Pilkington, my replacement, was killed. I reflected on what kept me alive for so long in the bush. What was it? Was it me or my men? Was it a carryover from the TET offensive that got Lt. Pilkington? What got him and not me? Was it fate? What is God's plan for us? Why did I survive my bush time? Why couldn't he?

I had been notified that a platoon in Charlie Company had lost their commander. He had been severely wounded and had to be medevaced. I was being assigned back to the bush to take over that platoon. Charlie Company was in the Arizona Territory. I was not excited about going back to where there was nothing but bad-ass gooks.

It was late morning on May 20, 1969 and I was getting my pack ready to ship out to my new platoon. I had half a bottle of Jack Daniels and I was reaching for it to put in my pack. I was looking forward to those last few sips when I heard the first rocket pass over my tent. You have probably heard that sound in the movies, that whistle overhead followed by a thunderous boom.

Performing one of my duties (Paymaster) as Exec Officer of Headquarters & Support Company. We had a small exchange where Marines could use military scrip to purchase necessities like toothpaste, candy, etc. In more secure areas like Da Nang a Marine could even purchase a bottle of booze.

The Viet Cong had timed it perfectly. It was about 11:30 a.m. when the lunch mess call sounded. The mess call was a loud siren that let the camp know that chow was ready. This was the same siren that alerted the camp of an attack, so no one was alarmed or reacted when the siren went off. Within thirty seconds of the siren the first rocket whistled over my head. Everyone was out in the open heading for the mess hall. I dropped my bottle of Jack and wheeled around to head for the bunker outside the tent and dive into it. I took one step and felt a shock wave hit me in the face. At the same time the right side of my body was jolted and I spun around as if I had been hit with a baseball bat. I fell to the floor of the tent and started to crawl toward the opening. I knew I was hit on the right side, but I had no idea where. The jolt made me think it was high on the right side, somewhere near the hip, about belt high. I pressed as hard as possible with my right hand on my groin knowing that area was the location of a major artery. Then, using my left arm, I pulled myself to the open flap of the tent and down the three steps to the ground. There was no way I could make it into the bunker, so I just lay on the ground at the foot of the steps pressing on my groin and trying to stay low out of the shrapnel pattern in case more rockets landed nearby.

The attack was over in less than a minute. The volley of six rockets had come from the Arizona Territory about eight miles northwest. They proved to be Soviet 122 millimeter rockets, highly portable and stood about six feet tall. They could be fired quickly from tripods. Each warhead of the rocket had about sixty pounds of explosive with iron shrapnel.

The first Marine to reach me was Lieutenant Jacobson. He had a battle dressing in hand and started to tear it open with his teeth. Another Marine arrived as Jacobson was tending my wound. Jacobson ripped my trousers on my right leg to expose the wound. I could not bring myself to look at what had taken place. As Jacobson was applying the battle dressing I heard the other Marine say, "Tie the knot over the hole." Over the hole! I have a hole? My mind could not comprehend my body was violated with a "hole." The concept seemed so foreign to me; A HOLE?! Yet, I felt no pain whatsoever. It was like a dream and everything was moving in slow motion. My right leg was numb and shock eliminated any sense of pain.

Within minutes I was on a stretcher and placed on the back of a jeep headed for the helipad. The blades of the chopper spun rapidly as corpsmen loaded me and the other wounded on board. One of the corpsmen on the chopper gave me a shot of morphine. I did not feel it was needed, but I did not argue. My leg felt like a lead weight attached to my body. I could not feel anything below the waist and I wondered if my leg was lost.

The chopper lifted off and I looked to my left. I saw another Marine on a stretcher next to me with his head completely wrapped in a blood-stained dressing that covered his right temple and looped repeatedly around his head, covering his eyes. Occasionally he would jerk uncontrollably as if an electric shock was being applied. I have no idea if he survived.

The chopper ride to Da Nang seemed to take seconds rather than minutes. It must have been a time warp caused by the morphine. The medical staff carried all of us wounded from the chopper and placed us on wooden slabs that tilted about 30 degrees with our heads elevated. There was a small trench at the foot of the wooden slab to catch the blood dripping off the slabs. Then a nurse using a scissor-like device started to strip us. First, she would cut through the laces of our boots, then up the trousers of each leg, through the belt, through the shirt and down each arm. It reminded me of skinning a deer. All my clothing was removed as well as the battle dressing on my leg. I was lying on a wooden slab on the tarmac of the Da Nang Airport buck naked with dozens of medical staff walking by as jets taxied past us for takeoff. Several of the medical staff were good-looking nurses. I felt a twinge of embarrassment.

Finally, I had the guts to look down at the result of what had violated my body and created "A HOLE." It was surprisingly simple. The hole was round, about the size of a fifty-cent piece. It was on the outside of my right thigh and did not appear to have hit the bone. The flesh surrounding the hole collapsed inward to form a crater the size of a golf ball. The exit wound on the back of my leg was not round. It was a slit about half an inch wide and one and a half inches long. The fragment had passed through the outer muscles. The impact was flat, as if a half dollar was placed on the leg, but as it passed through my leg it made a quarter rotation and came out edge first, making a slit. I felt relief that my leg would probably survive and forgot about my nakedness.

The shock of the cold water spray startled me and pissed me off. I couldn't figure out why some son-of-a-bitch was walking down a row of naked wounded soldiers on wooden planks spraying them down with a garden hose! My irritation was quickly recognized by one of the nurses. She informed me that they needed to spray us down to see if blood was oozing from other penetrations. Her explanation made sense and I dropped my head on the wooden plank as the second pass of cold water spray shrunk my manhood.

Finally, I was placed on a gurney and wheeled into a staging area for surgery. I don't remember how long I waited. It did not matter, because others had more serious injuries and I was still in a state of suspended animation (thank you, morphine).

When I was wheeled into the operating room I remember the surgeon lifting the knee of my injured leg and flopping it over my good leg. His action was clearly a move to survey the extent of the wound and identify the entry and exit of the shrapnel. His demeanor was matter-of-fact and straightforward. No doubt this was a daily routine for him. Then he asked me, "You wanna be awake or out for this?" "Put me out!" was the last thing I remember saying.

I awakened in a stiff military bed with tubes stuck in my arms. My leg was wrapped in gauze from the knee to my groin. There was no pain. I was not sure if the anesthetic was still working or if nerve damage from the wound had eliminated the pain. After a day or so that question was answered: it was numbness from nerve damage.

I remained in the Naval Aid Station, at the Da Nang Airport, for a couple of days. General Sparks stopped by to present me with my second Purple Heart and complete the photo op for my hometown newspaper. Although appreciated, I later felt this event to be overly publicized and routine as General Sparks moved from bed to bed through the Aid Station with his photographer.

In the afternoon of the third day I was placed on a cot and loaded onto a C-130 with about twenty other wounded Marines. Our destination was the Naval Hospital on Guam. It was explained to me that Guam was much better suited to perform the surgery necessary to close the wound and perform post-operative care.

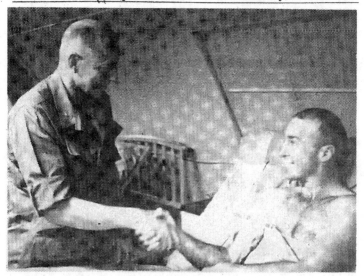

Two purple heart medals

General Sparks presented a second purple heart medal to First Lt. Frank A. Hill after he was wounded in the leg during shelling near DaNang May 20. He received his first purple heart for a slight wound in December.

Lieutenant Hill sustains second Vietnam wound

By Harriet Hixenbaugh

First Lt. Frank A. Hill, marine corps, has been wounded twice since he arrived in Vietnam in November.

He was wounded May 20 by shrapnel during a rocket shelling of a village outside DaNang. He was serving as executive officer of headquarters and support company at AnHoa.

Within minutes he was evacuated to DaNang and underwent surgery for extensive muscle and tissue injury in the right thigh. He has been transferred to a hospital at Guam and hopes to be moved to a hospital in Honolulu where Mrs. Hill has been living since his rest and recreation leave in March. She is the former Miss Diana Nolon of 900 Applewood av., a 1965 Littleton high school graduate.

Hill, a 1963 LHS graduate, received a purple heart medal earlier for a shrapnel wound he sustained Christmas eve. It was a slight wound, and he didn't miss a day of combat. He was in combat until March 1, according to Mrs. Carl L. Nolon, his mother-in-law.

We arrived at the Guam Naval Hospital late in the evening. The hospital ward was an old building with ten beds along each wall across from each other. Each bed had an overhead rack with mosquito nets that draped down over the bed. Evidently mosquitoes carried malaria in Guam as well as Vietnam. However, rather than relying on the malaria pills issued in Nam, we now had to rely on the mosquito nets.

There was no pain in my leg when a couple of nurses arrived at my bedside. Their demeanor was methodical, with little inclination to comfort. Again, this was a daily routine for them. They announced their arrival with, "We need to change your dressing." As they unwrapped the gauze from my leg I could see a large piece of gauze jammed into the side of my leg. "Wait a minute!" I thought, "This can't be right. I had a hole, not the side of my thigh missing." Then one of the nurses started to pull the gauze out of the open wound. Where there was previously no pain instantly turned into unbelievable, excruciating trauma that felt like someone was trying to amputate my leg on the spot. I grabbed the bed rail above my head, gritted my teeth, and withheld the expletives swimming in my mind. Finally, the gauze broke free and I could see the result of the surgeon's work in Da Nang. What was once a simple hole in the top of my thigh was now a slash from the entrance of the wound around the outside of my thigh to the exit point on the back of my thigh. I felt like the surgeon must have been a butcher in a previous life! He slit my thigh from the front to the back exposing the path of the shrapnel through my leg. It seemed like a lumberjack could have hit me with an axe about six inches below the hip and made a better cut.

Once the gauze was removed I was once again free of pain. It was amazing to see this wound with no anesthetic and not feel any pain. Yup, the nerves were gone. It reminded me of going to the supermarket and looking at a prime piece of beef steak! It was not bleeding, not quivering, nothing. It was just raw flesh. Then the nurses poured a fluid on the wound that was brown

In my bed at Naval Hospital on Guam just before the wound was closed. Notice the bottle of antiseptic by my side that looked like Worcestershire Sauce.

like Worcestershire sauce, but smelled like alcohol. They left the wound open and free to "breathe." I didn't care. It was late. I was tired and I lapsed into blissful slumber in minutes.

The next day the nurses came by and lifted the bed sheet to review the gap in my leg. They brought forceps and scissors. I was uncertain as to their intent. Then they lifted a piece of flesh inside the wound and clipped it off, then a second and a third. There was no pain. The meat was dead and they had to clean the wound of the dead tissue. Now I understood why the surgeon sliced my leg open!

One of my ward mates could not believe I was smiling while the nurses cut and probed in my leg. Little did he know the nerves were shot to hell. He asked if he could take a picture. I said, "Yes, but you have to send me a copy." He agreed.

For the next three to four days this routine of clipping dead flesh from the wound continued. Then a Naval surgeon came to my bedside and informed me that the next day he would close

165

the wound. He said I would be able to request pain medication every four hours. My initial thought was, "Big deal, I've had my leg laid open like a filet mignon for a week with no pain killers."

As I was wheeled into the operating room the next day they gave me a spinal anesthetic. As I drifted off I could sense the rocking motion of the surgeon using what I envisioned was a wire brush scraping off the last remaining bits of dead flesh in the wound. I'm sure he needed to get down to new flesh in order to bond and ultimately close the gap in my leg.

I awoke back in my bed. It felt like my leg was attached to a tractor trying to pull it off. Pain?...are you kidding me? Holy shit! It was incredible. I raised my arm and the corpsman on duty came to my bedside asking what was needed. I requested something to kill the pain. He returned and gave me a shot in the arm. I didn't know what it was and I did not care. I lapsed into unconsciousness. Within what seemed like minutes I awoke again with that tractor still pulling on my leg. My hand raised and the corpsman did not need to ask what was needed. He arrived with another shot and this one went in my thigh. This routine continued for a couple of days, rotating shots between thighs, arms and butt.

A day after the surgery to close the wound, a nurse changed the dressing wrapped around my thigh. It was an interesting sight to see silver steel wires sticking out of my leg. I expected to see stitches like any closed cut would have, but instead there were long twisted wires every half inch that looked like miniature spikes protruding from my thigh!

One night I forgot to drop my mosquito net and awoke with swarms of mosquitoes feasting on me. It seemed unusual that no one in the ward dropped the mosquito net, but another shot was administered and I lapsed back into blissful sleep.

Having spent seven days on Guam, I was informed I would be sent to Tripler Army Medical Center in Honolulu to complete recovery and undergo physical therapy. This news

WESTERN UNION
TELEGRAM

CLASS OF SERVICE
This is a fast message unless its deferred character is indicated by the proper symbol.

SYMBOLS
DL = Day Letter
NL = Night Letter
LT = International Letter Telegram

The filing time shown in the date line on domestic telegrams is LOCAL TIME at point of origin. Time of receipt is LOCAL TIME at point of destination

1030P PDT MAY 22 69 LB442 KA036

R-DVB589 (SY WA318) XV GOVT PDB 2 EXTRA FAX WASHINGTON DC VIA
DENVER COLO 22 LORENE S HILL, DONT PHONE CHECK DLY CHGS ABOVE
75 CTS
    DONT DLR BTWN 10 PM AND 6 AM LOCAL TIME 950 MERIDIAN AVE
#59 SANJOSE CALIF
THIS IS TO INFORM YOU THAT YOUR SON FIRST LIEUTENANT FRANK A HILL USMC
WAS INJURED ON 20 MAY 1969 IN QUANG NAM PROVINCE, REPUBLIC
OF VIETNAM. HE SUSTAINED A FRAGMENTATION WOUND TO THE RIGHT
THIGH FROM HOSTILE ROCKET FIRE WHILE IN A DEFENSIVE POSITION.
HE IS PRESENTLY RECEIVING TREATMENT AT THE STATION HOSPITAL,
DANANG. HIS CONDITION AND PROGNOSIS WERE BOTH GOOD. YOUR ANXIETY
IS REALIZED AND YOU ARE ASSURED THAT HE IS RECEIVING THE VERY
BEST OF MEDICAL CARE. IT IS HOPED THAT HE WILL COMMUNIIATE
WITH YOU SOON INFORMING YOU OF HIS WELFARE. HIS MAILING ADDRESS
REMAINS THE SAME. HIS WIFE, FATHER, SISTER, AND JOHN HILL HAVE
BEEN NOTIFIED
    LEONARD F CHAPMAN JR GENERAL USMC COMMANDANT OF THE MARINE
CORPS.

was fantastic. Diana had remained in Hawaii after our reunion for R&R. She was well-informed concerning the wound and my condition, as were our families back home. I was interested in how she heard about my wound and asked her to tell that side of the story. She was working in a deli in Kailua Kona, a tourist town on the big island of Hawaii. A young Marine in uniform was sent from Pearl Harbor to notify her in person. As he walked into the deli Diana could see he was anxious about how to deliver the news. So she spoke first and said, "I already know Frank was wounded and well cared for. Sorry you had to make the trip from Pearl." Notification for severe wounds or death goes to the Marine's residence on record. This happened to be Diana's parents' address in Colorado, and her mom had called her as soon as she was notified. The Marine was relieved and informed Diana I would be sent to the Naval hospital on Guam. Diana asked about the possibility of her going to Guam, but the Marine said "It is possible Lt. Hill could be sent to Tripler Medical Center on Oahu."

Little did I know she had been in daily contact with the Marine Attaché at Pearl Harbor asking if they could help her make the trip to Guam. Because she was residing in Hawaii and I had sixty days of rehabilitation ahead they agreed to send me to Tripler.

Dear Diana,

It is 11:00 The 23 and this is The first time I have had a chance to write with all The needles and stuff Taken out. Well I'll give you The stright scoop. I got a hole in my right Thigh big enough to put your fist in. It is hard to write in this possition. It was a 122 rocket that hit about 15 yrds away. A chunk of shrapnel about The size of a golf ball

THE AMERICAN NATIONAL RED CROSS

hit me dead center in the leg. Fortunatly it came from my left front as I was facing the explosion 2nd so it missed the bone. But the muscle & tissue damage is pretty extensive. One Doctor said it would be two months before I'm back to normal. I should be limping around in about 10 days. They are letting it drain now and going to sew it up Monday. The inside of my leg looks like beef stake!

THE AMERICAN NATIONAL RED CROSS

Some of the other patients think I may be sent home. I don't know for sure but I believe it is possible. At any rate I'm not getting my hopes up for anything If they do send me back I'm going to beg for a job at Division. And if they do maybe you can fly down and spend the last few weeks in Guam with me. Then I'll ask for R & R in Sept. We'll fake 'em. Of course it would be much better if they first shipped me home!

THE AMERICAN NATIONAL RED CROSS

Everything else is fine I may lose some wt. or get a little puffy being layed up for so long but I'll get back in shape. So the best thing to do is stay put keep right on doing what you have been and wait until they decide what they are going to do with me. One way or the other we'll see each other in Aug or sooner. I'm kinda pooped so I'm going to sleep a bit. Now I miss you more than ever. I never knew how much you ment until that metal hit me. God I pray they don't send me back.

I love you

Frank

MAY 23, 1969 | GUAM NAVAL HOSPITAL | TYPESET PAGE 237

twenty four

RECOVERY AT TRIPLER

I was loaded onto a C-130 transport for the nine hour flight to Hawaii with twenty other wounded Marines. It would be an overnight flight. The cots, suspended three high and held by straps, that were attached to each side of the plane so they could be folded up to allow larger cargo to be loaded. The flight was pleasant and the medical staff checked frequently to ensure our comfort. Thankfully, I slept for the entire flight.

We landed in Honolulu at Hickam Air Force Base early the next morning and the medical staff loaded us, four at a time, on an ambulance to be transported to Tripler Army Medical Center. Tripler was a sprawling pink stucco building on a hill with a commanding view overlooking Pearl Harbor. It took less than ten minutes to drive from Hickam to Tripler Army Hospital. Once we arrived at Tripler, medics started to pull our cots off the ambulance. One medic asked if I could get off the cot and walk. His tone seemed sarcastic and degrading to me so I replied, "Hell, no, I can't walk! Why do you think I'm lying on this damn cot?" I had been on my back for almost two weeks and wasn't sure if I could stand, let alone walk. They wheeled me to my room and lifted me onto a bed.

I knew Diana was flying from the Big Island so she could be close to the hospital. The attending physician checked in on me and I asked, "My wife is here in Hawaii and I'd really like to be with her. When can I be released?" He replied, "When you can walk we will release you for outpatient therapy." Without hesitation I replied, "I can walk!" He said, "Okay, get up and let me see you walk down the hall." Although I hadn't been on my feet since the day I was hit, I was determined to show that I could walk - or at least limp. My left leg hit the floor first. The wounded leg was stiff and tight from the pressure of the stainless steel sutures holding the wound closed. Bracing myself on the bed, I stood with most of the weight on my good leg. Slowly I lifted my right leg and it felt like that tractor was pulling it off again. Down came my right foot and that tractor went away. I grabbed the rail on the wall and preceded down the hallway about twenty steps, turned and came back to my room. The physician said, "Fine, walk down to the administration wing and sign your release forms. You will be expected back here each morning and afternoon for rehab and physical training." "Great!" was all I could say as I tried to cover the pain with a faint smile.

I pressed the call button next to my bed and a medic arrived shortly. I told him, "I need my leg wrapped with a layer of cotton taped over these wire spikes sticking out the side of my leg." Wound or no wound, I was hornier than a young bull in a herd of heifers. No way was I going to have a bunch of wires sticking out of my leg getting in the way. The medic returned with the cotton and tape I had requested. He did a fine job wrapping my leg with gauze and encasing the steel wires in cotton.

I was issued a pair of crutches and was hobbling my way to the administrative wing of the hospital when Diana found me in the hallway. What a joy to see her smiling face. We hugged for a long time, kissed, and then I told her where I was headed. The administration office was in a remote wing of the hospital. That damn tractor was back, trying to pull my leg off with every step. Diana strolled with me as I slowly became use to limping with the crutches. We filled out the paperwork and returned to my room to collect my personal effects, a wallet, and some pills.

We left the hospital with me still wearing hospital clothing. I had no civilian clothes and can't remember how we acquired any, but we somehow did and I was happy to look like a normal person in civvies.

Diana had rented a car and a place to live near the hospital for the next few weeks while I returned daily for physical therapy. The apartment she found was in a basement that had an outside entrance down concrete steps between two cinder block walls. The cinder blocks had a thin layer of green moss. It felt like going down into a root cellar where a farmer would store his potatoes for winter. Just inside the door to the left was a double bed and the bathroom to the right. There was no door to the bathroom, just a curtain to pull for some privacy. A small kitchenette was on the far wall a few feet from the foot of the bed. The only natural light was from a small window near the ceiling over the bed. The view out the window was a bricked window well. For me it was like walking into the Grand Suite of the Ritz. The cotton padding on my leg performed well, and Diana survived without going to bed with a porcupine.

The next few days Diana drove me back and forth to the hospital for physical therapy and some shopping trips. The leg was improving rapidly, the "tractor" was gone. I could finally limp stiff-legged without using crutches. We decided to hit the Officer's Club at Fort Shafter for dinner and drinks. Since I couldn't drive I was free to lay on a few beers and make up for that bottle of Jack Daniels I left behind several weeks ago. I did not hold back. I think Diana almost had to carry me down the steps to our cramped basement apartment. I collapsed on the bed and don't remember my head hitting the pillow.

Early the next morning I had to pee like crazy. When I got up the room felt cold and I was chilled to the bone. Dizziness came over me as I got out of bed and took that first step. I placed one hand on the wall in front of me to steady myself as I straddled the toilet. I noticed my urine was not a normal clear yellow, but rather a milky pale yellow. Something was definitely wrong. My first thought was blood poisoning from the wound. I staggered back to the bed and told Diana what was going on and said, "We need to go back to the hospital now!" She was not sympathetic with her reply, "I think you have a hangover." Her response was understandable and much warranted. I had really tied one on the night before and that was certainly aggravating whatever else was going on.

The sun was just coming up when we arrived at Tripler. We checked in and a nurse drew blood. After a few hours came the news from the doctor, "Lieutenant Hill, you have malaria! You will need to remain here for treatment." I had just arrived in a civilized place, spent three nights with my wife and now this! I was upset. "How long will that take?" I asked in a frustrated voice. The doctor replied, "At least one week, maybe two."

The chills started. It felt like walking outside naked on a cold winter night, yet my temperature was approaching 104 degrees. How could this be? I was burning up inside and all I wanted was a blanket. Instead, I was placed in a bathtub of ice, given medication and told to relax! Yeah, right.

Diana visited me for the next ten days while I was being treated for malaria and continuing physical therapy. I felt fine after the first few days of treatment. My leg was mending and the fever was gone. I couldn't understand why I needed to be confined for another week. I was told the medication had to be administered consistently around the clock.

Diana did not like staying in that damp, creepy basement apartment by herself, so she searched for a week-to-week rental that was above ground. With the assistance of the housing department at Pearl Harbor she found a nice little flat above a grocery store in a shopping mall, just off the main road not far from Tripler.

In June both my parents, who had been divorced, wanted to visit us in Hawaii. Dad came first. For a man who was never without a suit and tie I was shocked that he adorned himself with bright pink trousers and a matching pink & white tropical

Dad visiting us in Hawaii

shirt. I almost did not recognize him. We enjoyed dinners in his hotel, visiting some tourist attractions, relaxing and watching the sunsets.

Mom arrived shortly after Dad left and she took on the same free spirit as one would do visiting a tropical paradise. She wore a brightly-colored muu muu, put a lily in her hair and we all went to a luau. Mom and Diana fed off each other, enjoying as much sightseeing as possible. I complied with the hectic pace, but was getting worn out.

After Mom returned to the states, Diana and I started relaxing on the beach at Waikiki. My right leg was still bandaged, but I was wearing swimming trunks and enjoying the sun. A young man who was walking on the beach noticed my bandaged leg, came up to us and asked, "Frank! Lieutenant Hill?" By crazy coincidence, it was Lieutenant Jacobson who was the first to attend to my wound in An Hoa. Jacobson was on R&R with his wife. We had a great conversation reminiscing about that fateful day when the rockets exploded around us. I am not sure the girls appreciated the conversation laced with testosterone.

By mid-July the leg had mended well. I was back to normal except for numbness on the right side of the thigh. I could not feel anything from the wound down the leg for about eight inches. The doctor used a needle to poke around the wound to define the area of numbness. The nerves never came back, but I could walk without a limp. (Damp cold weather continues to aggravate the wound with a deep ache where the scar tissue reaches almost to the bone.)

It was time to be released back to active duty. I reported to the Marine Corps Depot at Pearl Harbor the next day with the medical papers issuing my release. The staff sergeant on duty took my papers, flipped through a number of pages on a clipboard, fumbled through some other documents on his desk and said, "Lieutenant, your flight to Da Nang will depart in two days at 1100 hours." My heart sank. I had heard that wounds requiring evacuation from Vietnam would be considered as completing that tour of duty in a combat zone. I questioned the sergeant, asking, "I thought evacuation with a severe wound completed the tour?" He was very blunt in his reply, "Sir, that is only if you have ninety days or less left on your tour. You have ninety-two days left." There was no more to be said. I got an issue of green Marine Corps fatigues and walked out of the office.

I told Diana I needed to return to Nam to complete my tour, which would end in November. Like me, she was disappointed. We discussed her plans. It was unlikely she could return to her job in Kona. She needed to collect her belongings from her roommates' house and say her goodbyes before returning to Colorado. She returned to Kona, spent a week packing and wishing others well and caught a flight home to Denver.

 DIANA'S REFLECTION PAGE 211

Diana and I enjoying a luau during leg rehab.

Picking up my Mom at Honolulu Airport.

DA NANG WAS NO PICNIC

Thankfully, leaving from Hawaii, the return flight to Nam was much shorter than the initial flight from California. I reflected back on that first flight and how strange it seemed to be on a commercial airline delivering troops to Da Nang. Having experienced the massive military complex and security at the Da Nang Airport, it was no longer a surprise to be on a commercial aircraft. As we landed, I could see the row of slanted wooden planks I bled upon just two months ago. I was glad to see that no one was occupying those planks at that moment.

We deplaned and boarded dark green military buses that shuttled us to Division Headquarters. Nothing had changed, nor had I expected it. The prostitutes remained on the street corners hoping to find a Marine willing to pay their price. Their call was familiar and rang out without concern for who heard it, "Hey, Maaween, yo wonta fookie?"

We stopped at a gate manned by MPs (Military Police). The concertina wire was three rows high around the compound of Division Headquarters. The only buildings in the compound were Quonset huts, half round metal shells arranged in rows. We formed a line at the door with its red sign above: 1st Marine Division Personnel Headquarters. They called us in one at a time. All I possessed was the clothes on my back and my personnel folder. The Marine behind the desk was a Captain. By now I had been promoted to 1st Lieutenant, one grade below Captain, but there was no insignia on my uniform to identify my rank. I stood at attention and handed him my personnel folder. Knowing the policy to rotate platoon commanders out of the bush after six to eight months of combat, I asked, "Hey skipper, are there any jobs here at division?" He lifted his head. When his eyes met mine his stare was so contemptuous I could read his thoughts, "You chicken-shit son-of-a-bitch. You're just checking in and already want a job at division?" As he flipped open my folder I said, "Look, Skipper, I've spent eight months in An Hoa and the Arizona Territory. I've been whacked twice and I don't want my third heart!" As he looked at my record and verified my statements his demeanor did an about face. He knew that An Hoa and the Arizona were two of the meanest places in the Division's area of responsibility. He lifted his head and his gaze was one of gratitude, not contempt, and he said, "I've got just the job for you. I'll try to get you a job in G-5, Psychological Operations."

I felt a flurry of conflicting emotions. I was glad I was not going back to the bush. Three months was too short a time to get comfortable with a new platoon in combat situations. On the other hand, I would miss not being in a command position and calling the shots. Having spent the first seven months in the bush and being wounded in An Hoa, I was very much hoping to get assigned to a job in the "rear." When that became a reality I felt some sense of relief, but little did I know the challenges of the job and the risks involved would be every bit as dangerous as the bush with less control than I had when I led my own platoon in combat.

The amenities at Division surpassed those in the bush. We had showers, hot meals, movies, and a club to have a drink and relax. But the ever-present threat of attack remained and the sudden mobilization to participate in a fire fight occurred with regularity. The situation was a roller coaster of emotions: feel secure and relaxed, then fight, relax, fight. At least in the bush you had to be in a constant state of readiness. Never did you let your guard down. You knew the capability of the men fighting next to you. Not so in the "rear." I never knew the men, nor their capabilities, whom I would be leading into a fight. The sudden jolt to go fight while I was enjoying a relaxing moment intensified the anxiety.

With only three months left on my tour in Vietnam I was initially looking forward to my new job, Administrative Officer for Psychological Operations (psy-ops). It was called "G-5" for the fifth department reporting to the General. Although I knew nothing about psy-ops, I had a staff of clerks who had been working in G-5 for many months and they knew what the commanding general was interested in accomplishing. The strategy I adopted for managing my responsibility in G-5 was no different than taking over a new platoon in the bush. The best approach was to let the men teach me. They knew the "terrain" and what to expect. They had experience with the enemy and they knew their tactics. I would make the final decisions, but I would consider everyone's input. So I had a one-on-one meeting with everyone in the office. I asked each of them for his advice and what he needed from me to be successful in acquiring the information the General wanted. (See Appendix for Military Ranking)

Unfortunately, the head of G-5 and my commanding officer, Colonel Faro, was a tough guy to work for. It seemed nothing made him happy. I don't think his vocabulary included "thank you" or "nice job." He was on my case constantly, and I'm sorry to say I reflected some of his callousness to my men. I harshly demanded that the reports from prisoner interrogations and propaganda be delivered on time and well documented. One of my responsibilities was to brief the commanding General in his weekly staff meeting. Statistics regarding propaganda leaflet drops and details regarding how many Vietnamese responded to the rewards or sanctions being

Standing in front of my Quonset hut office at
Division Headquarters, Da Nang. G-5 (sign under window)
was the organization responsible for intelligence.
We compiled information from prisoner debriefings,
organized leaflet drops to promote and reward
information from the general population.

offered for information were main points of each briefing. I
hated having to brief the General. These made me more
nervous than getting into a fire fight. I didn't know what to
expect. At least in a fire fight I knew where the enemy was and
how to engage them. It was so different to walk into a room with
a bunch of senior officers smoking cigars, looking at you with
condescending stares, and not knowing what questions would
be asked of you. I felt completely out of my comfort zone.

Life within the Division compound was better than An Hoa,
but not by much. We enjoyed hot meals and showers and slept in
corrugated tin-roofed hooches with wooden floors raised on stilts
to avoid the mud. Taking rocket fire was an ever-present threat just
like it was at An Hoa. Having sustained a rocket wound once, in a
similar compound, I was not willing to take the risk of having to run

to a bunker again. I stacked a pile of sandbags next to my cot. The stack was two bags high and about six feet long. All I had to do was roll off my cot and lie among the sand bags. The only way a rocket could get me would be if it hit the tin roof over my head. I can only recall having to dive into my self-made bunker two or three times during rocket attacks at night. Fortunately, none of the explosions came close to our hooch.

One of the Quonset huts in the compound was designated the "Officers' Club." We could go there after dinner, watch movies and have a couple of drinks. The enlisted men had their club as well. It seemed odd to me to have separate clubs in a war setting after having spent so much time in the bush developing a special bond with my men. It was just like back in the states where the social life was separated between officers and enlisted Marines. On special occasions I remember sharing a beer or two with my men in the bush. It was no big deal and you either had their respect or you didn't.

The Division compound was situated on the eastern slope of a mountain just west of Da Nang. Although called a mountain it was only 1000 feet high. The steep slopes made it difficult to hike to the top. To my surprise it was a picturesque setting. The view to the east overlooked the city of Da Nang, its harbor, the air strip and out to the deep blue of the South China Sea. Unfortunately, the top of the mountain created vulnerability. If VC or NVA got to the top, they could easily fire rockets and mortars into the compound. Adding to this vulnerability was little protection on the other side of the mountain. The far west side was referred to as "Charlie Sector." It was not named after Charlie Company, but rather after VC and NVA, whom we also referred to collectively as "Charlie." That side of the mountain was noted for lots of VC/NVA movement. Occasionally a patrol would sweep Charlie Sector, but rarely did they turn up anything during their sweep. It was at night when the gooks ("Charlie") tried to move through the sector to rocket the compound.

To protect the compound during the night, a company of

men was formed called the "Reaction Company." It was not a full-fledged combat company; it was little more than a couple of platoons, maybe around seventy men at most. The Reaction Company was made up of clerks, cooks and a couple of infantry lieutenants like me. Although most had not been hardened by the bush, they were capable riflemen. (The philosophy of the Marine Corps was that every man, regardless of his job, was first and foremost a rifleman.) On frequent occasions I was called to lead one of the platoons of the Reaction Company during the night to secure the top or far side of the mountain and prevent VC/NVA from firing rockets into the compound. The Reaction Company could also be called out at a moment's notice to help with fire fights that broke out near the compound.

On one occasion the Reaction Company was called out to protect the compound by spending the night along a road on top of the mountain. It was after supper when we headed out. We reached the top just when the sun was setting. It was a stunning view of the Da Nang harbor. I almost forgot that a war was going on. There was no need to set up a circular perimeter since the compound protected our back side. So we set in as a line on the road facing down the west slope. The moon was full and we had good visibility for a hundred yards or more. My radio man and I lay down on the edge of the road and I fell sound asleep. It was early morning when I woke up. It was still dark and my right thumb was throbbing. Something had bitten or stung my thumb during the night. As I rolled over to sit up it was evident what had attacked my thumb. There lay a squashed centipede about four inches long and the size of my finger. I couldn't believe how big it was. Later I found out they could get up to up to six inches long! Other than my wounded thumb it was an uneventful night and we descended the mountain as the sun started to rise over the ocean. It was beautiful!

Dearest Diana,   1900 24 Aug.

It has been a long day. It started at 05:00, when Capt. Milici came storming into my hootch. The lines were getting hit in Charlie sector and the reaction Company was being called out. Well, we got saddled up and moved out. Our mission was to seal off the avenue of escape by trucking around the mountain to a blocking position. I went with the first plt. and set in a block facing the ridgeline that had been attacked, while another company sweeped down the slope. F-4 fantoms were called in and one of our men was hit by a bomb fragment just below the knee. It brock both bones and stuck in, half out and half in like the blade of a hatcet. When the corpsman got to him the metal was still so hot it was sizzling in his flesh. They poured cold water on him and medivacked him out. He will keep his leg but it will be a long time before he walks. When we returned we learned a Lt. was killed during the early morning fighting. He was killed not far from the same place where I slept in the road. I wonder if there is an angle on my shoulder? Anyway, we waited in our blocking positions for over 4 hr. roasting in the heat. Then came on in. tonite im still on reactionary but hoping nothing will happen.

I haven't even had time to learn the Generals brief for tomorrow. It will probably be a real lulu! If I keep this busy who needs to worry about time going fast. Everything is so damn quiet while I'm gone then all hell breaks loose when I return; it really ~~pisses me~~ pisses me off. Why? I'm glad I get off this reactionary Sept. 20 for R&R. I hate this getting set up all the time. In a way it is worse than the bush, because when they call you they are going to put you in the hottest spot. I got out of the frying pan into the fire! I just have the comforts of home here that is all. ~~~~ Fear is _inversly_ _proportionate_ to time remaining in vietnam! Understand? Time ↓ Fear ↑ And Thought of you and home are directly proportional.

AUGUST 24, 1969 | DA NANG | TYPESET PAGE 238

We got to the base of the mountain on the opposite side of the compound just as the sun was starting to come up. Fighting was taking place uphill from us and it did not seem to be all that intense. The bursts of automatic fire came every twenty or thirty seconds, not that constant roar of machine gun fire and explosions you would expect in a heavy fight.

Working up the hill in a column was not the best approach. Only three or four men in the front of the column could respond if we encountered enemy fire. So I formed a skirmish line with men side by side and about five yards between each man. Everyone was in sight of each other so cross fire casualty was less of a concern. We knew the objective was in front, not left, right, or behind. We started up the mountain.

I radioed the lieutenants of the other platoons in the Reaction Company and told them we had started our movement up the mountain. No one informed me that air support had been called in on the slope just above us. When we got about half way up the mountain I could hear the jets overhead. We had not taken any fire from the gooks ahead of us. Suddenly there was a series of huge explosions about two hundred yards up hill from us. Everyone dove face down on the ground. I heard that familiar whistle and flutter of shrapnel coming down as it landed in the bushes and trees around us. My mind flashed back to the Snake Eye bomb I blew up close to our position in the Horseshoe.

No one needed to call a corpsman. The scream was self-evident. I went toward the cry of pain, which was only fifty yards to my left. I arrived just after the corpsman and observed a shard of bomb shrapnel the size of a deck of cards embedded in the back of a Marine's leg. The shrapnel hit him in the calf muscle and was sticking out about two inches. There was little bleeding due to the flesh having been cauterized from the red hot metal. I felt sorry for him, but I did not dwell on his misfortune as I knew he would recover from his injury. Maybe having had a similar wound made me more calloused? I was angry someone had called in an air strike so close to our position without warning us. This was the problem with fighting with others who had not become familiar with each other's tactics, capability and coordination. I was second-guessing the wisdom of my desire to leave the bush.

In retrospect, the Division compound had lots of comforts of home - hot meals, showers, movies and beer. However, I hated having to be called out on "Reactionary." Every fight put you in the hottest spot and I did not know how my fellow lieutenants or the men I was leading would react. It was like being on a vacation and suddenly told to fight a battle. The transition was surreal. One moment you are watching a movie and having a beer and the next moment you are climbing a mountain and hoping a piece of shrapnel doesn't hit you. At times I felt I had made the wrong decision. Send me back to the bush where I knew my men and I knew what to expect. I trusted my fellow platoon commanders. I knew how to fight and lead my men in the bush! Unfortunately, with so little time left on my tour it would have been too difficult to become familiar with a new platoon. I had no choice but to hunker down and stick it out!

twenty six

GOING HOME

It was like having a bad dream and waking up to a new dawn. The landing gear lifted on the passenger jet as it departed from the Da Nang Airport in November, 1969. I did not feel joy or elation, but rather thankfulness for having survived, when my tour of duty ended. My thoughts focused on getting home, seeing Diana, and starting a new chapter in our lives together.

After a two-day layover in Okinawa, I began the final leg of my return journey to the United States. As expected, the flight was a commercial airline. Probably the same airplane that had delivered troops to Da Nang the day before was now on its return flight. The atmosphere on this flight was quite different from thirteen months ago when we were headed in the opposite direction. I saw men standing in the aisle chatting and laughing. The excitement and anticipation of going home fueled everyone with high spirits.

We landed at Travis Air Force Base near Sacramento, California. Since my sister's family and our father still resided in Sacramento, it made sense to spend some time there and catch up on all the relatives' lives. As much as I missed Diana and was looking forward to our reunion, flying her to California for a few days seemed too little a time and did not fit the budget. Besides, after our time apart, a few more days would make the homecoming that much sweeter without the distraction of my family.

Because all my uniforms had been stored in Denver, my travel attire for the final flight home was civilian. I was not concerned about being the target of the Vietnam War (Conflict?!) protestors and, thankfully, I did not experience any protests or demonstrations against me or other returning troops. If I had, I'm not sure how I would have reacted. I was proud of my service, but very happy to be home. I doubt I would have been confrontational. After all, the point of serving our country is to preserve those rights to demonstrate and speak freely.

My orders could not have been more straightforward, "Report to Naval Station, Norfolk, Virginia on December 1st, and take command of the Marine Detachment aboard the USS Wright." So Diana and I crammed everything we could into our two-door 1968 Dodge Charger and headed for the east coast. Our plan was to take a week visiting friends and relatives on the way. After visiting old high school friends in Wichita, Kansas, we pulled into Kansas City late at night, dragging our tails. We found a motel near the highway, went to our room and crashed in deep sleep. Upon waking early the next morning we discovered, to our dismay, that our car had been broken into and all of our clothing had been stolen, including Diana's wedding dress and all my uniforms. I couldn't believe the thieves missed the pistol that was stashed under the driver's seat. After filling out the police report and jamming cardboard into the broken car window, we proceeded on our way east. Thanksgiving with Diana's aunt and uncle in Illinois was a welcome stop. The remainder of the drive to Norfolk was thankfully uneventful.

The USS Wright was an aircraft carrier converted to serve as one of two ships for National Emergency Command Post Afloat (NECPA). The Wright's sister ship was the USS Northampton. In the event of a national emergency the

President and his Joint Chiefs of Staff would board either the Wright or the Northampton, which would sail to an undisclosed location while the President and his staff directed operations to address the emergency.

Jim Winch was my Executive Officer of the detachment. I had the utmost respect for Jim. We had both served in Vietnam and each of us had been medevaced from the field. Jim was an artillery officer and had served as a Forward Observer in Nam, a difficult and dangerous job. Jim had my total trust as my backup. Since we both had responsibility for security aboard the ship, each of us had access to the combination for a safe that held our orders should the President come aboard. Fortunately, we never had to open that safe.

Life in Norfolk was dreary. It was December, 1969, and the sky was a persistent dull gray. Diana and I found a small furnished apartment on the shore of Chesapeake Bay near the Naval Station. The beach was less than a hundred yards away, but walking on it was bitterly cold as the wind chilled us to the bone when it came blowing off the water. My first order of business was to replace my stolen uniforms. Fortunately, I found a retiring Marine officer who was willing to sell his uniforms and, as luck would have it, we were the same size. Our only friends were Jim Winch and his wife, Karen. They, being from Texas, and we from Colorado, greatly missed the sunshine and blue sky of our home states.

We soon found that our tour in Norfolk would be short-lived. The USS Wright was scheduled to be decommissioned in a few months and placed in "mothballs" (retired and stored in a naval shipyard). It was determined that putting the President on a slow-moving ship out in the middle of the ocean was not a good idea and made for an easy target. As a result, the President would now retire to a jumbo jet fitted with the same global communication capability. That jet could be refueled in the air and remain airborne until the emergency was resolved. This new program was named NEACP (National Emergency Airborne Command Post).

With only one year left on active duty I was surprised to be presented with the option of choosing my next duty station, but it had to be in the United States. Diana and I had our fill of the wintry gray cold of the east coast and were ready to head west. That led us to select the sunniest duty station the Marine Corps had to offer, Marine Corps Air Station, Yuma, Arizona. Yuma needed a Station Athletic Officer to run their athletic programs and maintain the station's recreational facilities. I was excited about this new role. So in March, 1970, after spending the heart of winter on the Virginia coast we packed our bags, loaded the Dodge Charger again and headed for Arizona.

Yuma was the perfect place to end the remaining year of our military life and transition to civilian life. As the Station Athletic Officer I travelled with the base teams to regional inter-service competition in San Diego, Phoenix and Tucson. When possible Diana would tag along and we enjoyed the travel together throughout the southwest, supporting the Marine Corps teams. I remember one excursion where Diana and I drove from Yuma to Tucson in mid-summer in a pickup truck from the station motor pool. The truck had no air conditioning and the temperature was over 115 degrees. As we drove across the desert we rolled down the windows, stripped to our T-shirts and sprayed each other with a spray bottle to stay cool.

After spending a couple of months in an apartment off base and acquiring some furniture, we moved into base housing for married officers, a simple two-bedroom duplex. Orange groves flourished beyond our backyard and we welcomed the refreshing fragrance of their blossoms. Solid friendships developed with our neighbors, Vicki and Bob Russell, who have remained lifelong friends. We enjoyed exploring the desert on our motorcycle and free movies at the base theater. San Diego was a three hour drive away; we camped in the mountains on our way there. Life was good and the pain of war seemed a distant bad dream.

Three months before I was scheduled to be discharged I

was promoted to Captain. It felt good to have this promotion recognize my service and I considered making a career of the Marine Corps. However, extension would have certainly resulted in another tour in Vietnam. The thought of separation and the awareness of the pain of an inexhaustible war gave me pause, and I declined to extend. Diana heartily agreed!

The fall of 1970 brought a surprise: Diana was pregnant! Our first child was expected in May of 1971, one month after our release from active service. The timing meant we would pay for the delivery of our first child. Unknown to me, Diana had been saving money in anticipation of taking a trip to Europe. It was certain her stash would go toward paying the hospital bills. Having no job, a baby on the way, and wondering where we would live made me a bit anxious about our future!

I got a call from a recruiter for Electronic Data Systems (EDS) a month before we transferred out of the Marine Corps. He explained that EDS was a data processing firm and they needed computer professionals. "What? Me, a computer professional?" All I knew how to do was lead Marines. I quickly told him I knew nothing about computers and wished him good luck.

April arrived and Diana looked like she had a beach ball under her dress. Movers picked up what little furniture we had and we packed the car full of clothes and headed home to Colorado, not knowing what awaited us. I might have embraced a gypsy life if I could have been more of a romantic, but having a pregnant wife and no job concerned me. We moved in with Diana's parents in Littleton while we searched for a place of our own. The rental market was tight and it was difficult to find a place that we could afford. We went to the local newspaper office and grabbed a paper as it came off the press. Fortunately, we found a small two-bedroom duplex and began cleaning and painting it. Now that we had an address the movers could deliver our furniture. Diana overdid it while unpacking and her water broke that night. Earlier than expected, May 11, 1971,

Stephanie Ann Hill was born. She had ten toes, ten fingers. I was thankful for this healthy baby and mesmerized by the miracle.

My cousin, Leonard, worked for the Denver Water Board. With his help I was able to land a summer job reading water meters. The wage was one-third of my Marine Corps pay and barely covered the cost of rent or putting food on the table. My ego was taking a real blow. Here I was, reading water meters after leading forty men in combat, making life and death decisions and being responsible for the possibility of Presidential security aboard an aircraft carrier. Something had to change and it did! After four months of working for the Water Board I got a follow-up call from another EDS recruiter. He asked if I wanted to meet him at a hotel near Denver's Stapleton Airport. What could I lose? "You bet'cha, when do you want me there?" was my reply. I'd never had a computer course in college, but I was willing to look at anything to get out of reading water meters.

I met the recruiter in his hotel room. I expected to have an exchange of questions, but he sat me down at a table, placed a booklet in front of me and said, "Take this test." After about an hour I handed him the test and he graded it on the spot. When he had completed scoring my effort he lifted his head, looked at me with an expression that appeared to be a mixture of puzzlement and concern. My thought was, "Okay, I blew it. Let's get this over with." Then he asked, "Do you know what a flowchart is for?" "No" was my response. Then he explained, "A flowchart provides a logical path for a step-by-step decision process to solve a problem." I'm thinking, "Oookay, so what?" He recognized my body language as not putting two and two together and said, "You scored very low on technical under-standing, but your logic profile is exceptionally good. I want to send you to Dallas for a final interview." All I could say was, "Thanks! When should I go?" He said, "I'll make the reservation and let you know." What he said next gave me pause and concern. "When you finish your interview in Dallas you will be either offered a job or thanked for coming." "Okay" I thought, "I can deal with that." Then he said, "If you are offered a job, you have to accept or decline on the spot." I'd already made up my mind and knew if someone was interested enough to fly me to Dallas for an interview, the offer had to be better than reading water meters. Upon reflection I wondered if my degree in Physical Science helped with my logic score on the test.

A week passed and I received my ticket to fly to Dallas. Frankly, I can't remember much about the sprawling grounds of the EDS compound, except that it was impressive. In contrast, as I walked into the interview room I was surprised to find the room bare and intimidating, similar to a police interrogation room. The interview started at a long table with three men sitting opposite me. Questions came from them like a water spout: "What's the hardest decision you have ever made?" "How did you handle defeat?" "What has impressed you the most?" Then the most important question came with an elitist tone, "Why do you think you are good enough to be an EDS'er?" By now I was getting impatient and tired of this third degree. I leaned forward in my seat and replied, "What makes you think EDS is good enough for me?" I knew I had blown the interview. I did not care. I was challenged and let them know where I stood. After they left the room and convened for a few moments the three interviewers returned and said, "We want you to work for us!" I could not believe it. I was offered a job that exceeded my Marine Corps salary. Did I hesitate? NO! Thus began my computer systems development career.

Initially I was assigned to projects in Denver as I learned the ins and outs of customer service and how to develop requirements for systems development. After about a year we moved to Dallas, and I attended a rigorous training course to become a programmer. Diana and I made great friends with other former military officers and their wives, who had also been recruited by EDS. The strategy of hiring military officers struck me as a brilliant way to build a company. They were trained in leadership and accustomed to moving to new locations, as well as family separation.

I met Ross Perot, the founder of EDS. I was very impressed with his warm and engaging personality. We remained in Dallas after graduating from programmer training. Our son, Frank Dustin, was born there in September, 1973. Three months later we were assigned to Hartford, Connecticut, supporting EDS contracts with large insurance companies. Our home roots still beckoned us to return to Colorado. That, along with the notification of my mother's terminal lung cancer, gave us the incentive to leave EDS and make the journey back to Colorado in 1977.

 DIANA'S REFLECTION PAGE 212

twenty seven

THE AFTERMATH

We live in a sterile society. A walk in your neighborhood is done without surveying every step you take in the hope you don't set off a booby trap. Drawing a drink of water from the kitchen tap is taken for granted until you have had to fill your canteen from a murky river after waiting for a dead body to float by. Turning on the stove to heat soup is a casual event compared to warming a can of beans over an ignited ball of plastic explosive; closing the door to the restroom and flushing the toilet versus squatting a few feet off the trail within sight of forty men; watching a movie depicting violence with a sense of unrealistic detachment compared to watching the convulsive shaking and hearing the groaning death rattle of a dying comrade. Yes, we live in a sterile society.

War is like living in a cesspool. At first the stench of napalm and death is incomprehensible. Observing killing is repulsive and frightening. The enemy is feared. As time passes, experience and acclimation become the ultimate survival mechanism. That smell becomes commonplace and expected. Killing and death is just another day of work. At times death is considered a better option than living. Hate for the enemy replaces fear of them.

In the spring of 1975 the news broke with vivid realization that South Vietnam had been taken over by the North Vietnamese. I remember watching the news clips of that last helicopter taking off from the roof of the U.S. Embassy in Saigon showing people clamoring to get aboard. A sense of abandonment and betrayal fueled anger in me that we had just flushed over 58,000 American military lives down the drain. This anger soon changed to regret knowing this was the first war America had lost. Reflecting on my time in the bush, confirmed my view that we did not know, or learn, how to fight a protracted guerilla conflict. Our enemy knew that Americans had no appetite for supporting a continuous never-ending war and if they held on, domestic pressure to end it would be their greatest ally. To their credit, this strategy worked. Now as we enter a new era of protracted wars, we have a new dynamic impacting our ability to bring resolution to the conflict. It is not our disenchantment with a war, but rather our complacency for war. We do not have any investment in war. We are not sacrificing with a draft or rationing. We are insulated from the effects of war while we rack up a huge national debt to keep that insulation in place. We don't care, and war goes on. We have learned little!

How does war affect a person? Do you know if war has changed you? How will you find out?

Fast forward 12 years. The Hills have become a typical middle class suburban family. I am well established as a systems development manager. Diana has obtained her degree in design and works part time as a space planner for home remodeling. Stephanie is breaking into her teens and Dusty, our son, is involved with sports and Scouting. We have become regular church attendees and life is good. But is it? Really? For some there are hidden dangers.

The danger is hidden under the surface. It is silent and lurking like a shark searching for its next victim. Then, it surfaces, still unrecognized and hidden within the deep recess of our memory. After World War II the term to describe it was "shell shocked." Today Post Traumatic Stress Disorder (PTSD) has become a common term in our society. PTSD does not have to be the result of war. Many people who have not been to war have been diagnosed with it. For example, an extended abusive relationship or an experience like 9/11 can result in PTSD. For me, it was the fear of losing a comrade. I would not let myself get close to a fellow Marine so I would insulate myself from the pain of loss if he got killed. It was the ultimate protection mechanism.

There is also a second hidden danger we can bring back from war. It is guilt. It surfaces as our life experiences from being reintroduced into a sterile society make us recognize how others suffered as a result of our decisions or actions, even if justified.

I ordered the attack on that village when we took fire from it. Based on my training it was logical and warranted. But when we entered the village all we had to show for our counter-attack was a young girl with a bullet hole in her chest. When I saw my beautiful young daughter at about that same age, the memory of that Vietnamese girl surfaced and haunted me with guilt. I could now identify with the joy that was taken away from another father and mother due to my actions, regardless of justification. I felt I did not deserve this beautiful little girl; thus began the emotional distancing. And though you think you are punishing yourself for your guilt, you are actually punishing everyone close to you through no fault of their own.

Rational thinking makes us unique creatures in this world, but rational thinking is not always conscious thinking. We unknowingly can rationalize within our subconscious. PTSD buries itself there. It is a paradox. You can't stand the pain of losing someone so you put up a shield to protect yourself. You don't let yourself get close to that person you love for fear of losing them. You withdraw into a cocoon of self-protection. So it was with my daughter, Stephanie. As she entered a particularly turbulent adolescence, I withdrew more. I feared exercising parental guidance and discipline would drive her away. Little did I know that living behind a vail of self-protection would also place a wall between relationships. That subconscious rationalization withheld something she needed, a father who nurtured, a father who protected, and a father willing to show love.

Finally, Diana said, "Enough! You two have to talk to a counselor." So we did. But we did not attend counseling sessions together. Each of us expressed our views, experiences and our feelings in private with our counselor. After about three months the diagnosis came: "Frank, you are a classic case of PTSD." I was not familiar with PTSD or its effect on people. As the counselor began describing some of the characteristics, I resisted the diagnosis, thinking, "No. That is not possible; I work hard to provide a good living. I love my family." Then my counselor focused on the pain of loss and the vail of protection PTSD provides through disengagement. I could no longer deny the diagnosis. The shoe fit. The recommendation was simple: stop distancing myself, deal with the struggles of parenting in a loving manner, and be a partner with Diana in raising our children. It sounded logical, but in reality I did not change overnight. It took many years to bridge the distance between Stephanie and me, but we overcame that void and now enjoy a strong father-daughter relationship built around trust, forgiveness and understanding.

Although I was diagnosed with PTSD I never sought help from the Veterans Administration. Maybe I should have, but I felt I had received the help I needed. I knew what I had to do. It was now up to me.

As for my guilt, it was not my counselor who helped me let go of that self-destructive remorse. It was my pastor, Rev. Gran Smythe. I recall the moment vividly. Sure, I knew Christ died for our sins. But it was not until I was emotionally drained and spiritually lost in my guilt that Gran's words reached me. I don't recall exactly what he said or how he said it, but his words touched my heart and helped me embrace the sacrifice Jesus made for me. I embraced God's forgiveness and let go of that guilt.

So, this is my story. It is not unique. It is shared by many of our men and women in uniform today. I wish for them that they have a loved one who recognizes their changes and encourages them to find their inner self, free of guilt and a willingness to expose themselves to life's pains and struggles, as did I with the encouragement of the one true love of my life, Diana.

Please see Author's comments regarding the Gulf War in a News Press Article on page 239.

DIANA'S REFLECTIONS

War happens to people, one by one.
MARTHA GELLHORN, THE FACE OF WAR

REFLECTION ON CHAPTER ONE
PREPARING TO GO

A bit of history...

Frank graduated in March, 1968, from Colorado State University, which was then on the quarter system. We had met exactly one year earlier in Geology Lab. We got engaged when he returned from the six week summer Platoon Leader's Class training in Quantico, and set the wedding date for four months later. He resumed fall quarter at CSU. I dropped out of the CSU Art Department, moved back in with my parents, and got a job in Denver. We needed to save some money, and I also had the opportunity to reconnect with some former high school girlfriends. Frank worked nights at a plastic factory in Ft. Collins making plastic grips for .45 caliber pistol handles, the same Colt pistol he would use later in Vietnam.

Both of us had grown up in Littleton, CO, when it was a one-high-school small town. Since he was two years ahead of me at LHS, we hadn't crossed paths there. Perhaps, because we shared those hometown "roots" and common memories, we were comfortable together from the beginning on those geology field trips. After a small wedding (where we served rock candy!) on the snowy day after Christmas, 1967, I ended up with the

"M-R-S. Degree" instead! Perhaps the nomadic life of a Marine wife taught me more than an art degree from CSU in the "big picture" of life, anyway.

After our Christmas break honeymoon in California, we lived in a cozy trailer during the cold winter quarter. Frank finished his last few classes, we both worked, went skiing, and enjoyed time with our friends whom we would be leaving soon. Frank did not attend his graduation. Receiving his Lieutenant's bars at his USMC Commissioning Ceremony was good enough for him. His ATO Fraternity brothers threw him one heck of a farewell party! We traded in his Chevy Impala 409 for a 1968 Dodge Charger, gold with a white vinyl top. We named it "Trigger," since it was the color of Roy Rogers' palomino, put it in gallop gear, and went off into the unknown.

On our way to Quantico, our first road trip of many together, we stopped at Mt. Rushmore in South Dakota. The view was completely covered in spring fog, and we never saw the famous mountain sculptures. The next day, as we traveled to Michigan to visit family there, the car radio announced that Martin Luther King had been killed and we drove through Chicago as riots began. I had never been east of Michigan, so the rest of the trip to Virginia was a new adventure in tumultuous times. The night we arrived in Quantico, we watched the 1968 Academy Awards best picture "In the Heat of the Night."

It was the first time in many years that I was not in school or working, and I took advantage of all those free days. Naively, I jumped right in to "being" a Marine wife living in base housing. Some of our neighbors were career Marines, some in training with Frank. One California wife of a Marine in Frank's class had gotten married just days before they came and was struggling with the long hours and her husband's exhaustion. It made me thankful that we had wisely married four months earlier. We shared the front porch with our new neighbors who were from Tennessee and had just graduated from Vanderbilt Law School. My drinking experience was mostly college Coors 3.2 beer, legal at 18 in CO. My new neighbor introduced me to martinis, which she served up almost every evening as we waited on our front porch steps for our tired husbands to return from training. Perhaps I was in training for the copious drinking that takes place on military bases? Figuring out military terminology, ranks, and insignias, and how to appropriately live in the Marine Corps Semper Fi culture, was another learning experience. I had the time to experiment with cooking and learned a lot, spurred on by Frank's appetite and his great appreciation of a home cooked meal. Another neighbor taught me to make lasagna (which I had never eaten) as her Italian mother-in-law had taught her. She had a new adorable kitten, and I ended up getting the runt of that litter, a crooked-tailed Siamese, Mickey, who shared many car trips and homes with us over his next seventeen years.

Virginia was incredibly hot and humid to us dry-land westerners. A young Marine in training died from heat exhaustion that summer. We bought a small window air conditioner for sleeping in our upstairs bedroom, but during hot afternoons I would hop in the Charger, crank up the AC, and explore the Virginia countryside. I discovered antique stores and roadside markets. A bus trip for military wives took us to a special tour of the White House. Frank and I drove to Washington, DC when we could get away. We remember seeing the movie "2001" in a theater near the massive Watergate - not quite yet infamous. One of Frank's fraternity brothers lived in Lancaster, PA, and we greatly enjoyed several weekend visits with our fellow Coloradoans. We had an old "portable" black and white TV that we rarely watched, but in June, when Bobby Kennedy was shot, it was on for days. It was the best of times; it was the worst of times. That event tipped toward worst.

Watching the Mad Moment from bleachers near the imitation Vietnam village was surreal. Sort of like watching a war movie on a giant live theater stage. We observers had mixed reactions; some rather gung ho, others in quiet thought.

Getting things in order and watching Frank say goodbye to

family and friends in Colorado and California was a blur of business, busyness and hanging on to optimisim by a thread. My contained emotions were so raw by the time Frank put $20 on the roulette table in Tahoe that even I was surprised by my reaction. Jolted, scared, sad, confused like never before. It didn't have so much to do with the loss of money as the symbolism of the gamble - jumping in big and losing it all in one spin.

Frank took me to the Sacramento airport and we said our goodbyes as I boarded the plane. I was thankful that his dad was the one to take him to his flight out of Travis Air Force Base, which must have been another difficult farewell. (A former "stewardess" who attended those flights to Vietnam on American Airlines spoke of her very silent and anxious passengers as they flew those many hours over the Pacific. She described the precautions they took while quickly landing and departing in Da Nang.) Of course, any time we tell a loved one goodbye, there is no guarantee that it won't be the last. But sending one off to war is a very different kind of goodbye, with an extra dose of love, courage, faith and hope needed. As the plane lifted into the air I put my face in my hands and began weeping quietly, the kind of cry that gives you a sore throat from holding it in, and sensed the uncomfortable quiet of those around me. It was a blessedly short flight to L.A. to see my sister and her new baby boy before returning to Denver. Her husband was a jet mechanic on an aircraft carrier in the Gulf of Tonkin and she was living with her in-laws in Studio City. It was a good distraction to meet my new nephew, commiserate with my sis, and be in a completely different southern California environment for a few days.

Mickey and I moved in with my parents when I returned to Denver. I got a job as a bank teller in Littleton. It was October, 1968. The Hong Kong flu took out many of us tellers for a week that fall. Frank's letters began to arrive, as I watched the gut-wrenching Vietnam war and American peace demonstrations play out every evening on television.

REFLECTION ON CHAPTER NINETEEN
FROM BUSH TO R&R TO BUSH

While I was working at the bank, a high school friend that I hadn't seen for years came to my teller window. She was living on the big island of Hawaii and was home to see her family for Christmas. A month later, she wrote and said she was moving into a house and needed roommates. Would I like to move there after R&R? How fast could I say yes! I packed some summer clothes, left my cat with my parents, and left winter behind.

R&R

I flew to Honolulu a day ahead, since the men would come in very early the next day. Women were housed in rooms at Fort De Russy, a military reserve and recreation area near Waikiki, because the men were to be bused there to meet their loved ones for four days. It was good to be with others in the same situation and share stories while we waited. Most of us North American winter women went to the beach to get a "tan" before our guys got there and some ended up with nasty sunburns. Yeouch! I had been warned about that so I was careful, although that sun felt mighty good coming from end-of-February Colorado, and I ended up pinkish.

A very tall hotel, in a room high enough for a vast view of the ocean, became our home for a few precious days. It was several blocks from the beach and in the heart of the tourist area. We enjoyed just being together and splurging on good restaurants with interesting and diverse food. Visiting the Arizona Memorial at Pearl Harbor was a must.

Our sense of time was completely off, having come from very different time zones. Just before sunrise on our first morning there, we were walking the few blocks to the beach in the quiet city when some popping sounds went off somewhere in the area. Frank suddenly vanished from my peripheral vision when he went from walking beside me to a low crouch on the sidewalk in an instant. What he took as gunfire was actually firecrackers being set off to scare birds off a building. It took us a while to walk off all that adrenalin as we watched the sun rise at Waikiki beach. Today, Frank does not remember that incident, but I will never forget it. I suspect many of these R&R reunions were somewhat awkward, because even though you have been communicating through letters for months, these were changed men since the last time you saw them. Although appreciative of the time together, saying goodbye and sending them back again was terrible.

Fortunately, I again had the distraction of a new adventure. I hopped on a plane with my two suitcases, and moved my place of residence to Kailua-Kona, Hawaii, where letters from Vietnam arrived several days faster than Denver, and we had no TV to watch the war. The music from "Hair" on Broadway was on the radio: "Let the Sunshine In" indeed! Age of Aquarius? Hmmm...

REFLECTION ON CHAPTER TWENTY TWO
A SMOKING LETTER

I was pretty shocked when I received this letter, but I completely understood how Frank must have felt. I had plenty of opportunities to have a romantic relationship with other men, but I wasn't at all interested or tempted, so I felt a little miffed at the accusation, and also sad that it had upset him. Frank didn't realize that I sure wouldn't be casually writing about anyone I was serious about. It was a time in Kona when there were hippies living on the beach, many people coming and going in the tourist town, and the Ports o' Call Deli, where I worked, was a place they would stop in and hang out. We gave discounts to the locals. The Hawaiians were not happy with the invasion by the mainland haole* drug users. In fact, my boss at the deli and several other guy-friends had great respect for Frank serving in Vietnam and were quite protective of me–and, therefore, Frank. As for Stuart, he was just one of many who lived in town for a while, and moved on. In this particular instance, a group of us had planned to go to the movies. There was an old theater in the next town up the mountain, and all but Stuart backed out at the last minute. Having no car, I was up for going anywhere when I could get a ride.

As I watched the drama in the lives of my single roommates and friends, I was often thankful that I was married and could just be an observer of their trials and tribulations. It was nice when one of them was dating a fisherman and we got lovely fresh fish in exchange for cooking it and inviting him to dinner. I was also friends with many local Hawaiians and would play card games with some of them on the lanai of the deli when I got off work. Two jobs and my friends kept me busy...and distracted.

* A Hawaiian term used for "foreigners", pronounced howlie.

REFLECTION ON CHAPTER TWENTY FOUR
RECOVERY AT TRIPLER

I had been on the phone daily with Pearl Harbor trying to figure out a way to get to Guam. Probably because our "home" was now listed as Hawaii instead of Colorado, Frank was sent to Tripler for eight weeks of therapy and recovery. I caught the Aloha Airlines jet from little Kona to big Honolulu, rented a car, and went straight to the housing office at Pearl Harbor where they were very helpful. By the time I headed for Tripler, it was a nightmare of rush hour traffic, and I clearly remember looking at that big pink building on the hill and taking FOREVER to get there. Seeing him in the hall of the hospital was such a huge feeling of relief and gratitude, I could hardly catch my breath. Then, when the malaria showed up, such a feeling of disappointment. But we spent our days at the hospital playing cards, dreaming about our future, and catching up on old movies at the little hospital theater. On the 4th of July, we went out to the Tripler parking lot to look over the city and watch the fireworks. Some kids at the edge of the pavement accidentally started a brush fire with sparklers, so the entertainment switched from fireworks to fire trucks! Later that month, July 1969, we watched the lunar landing and moonwalk on TV in the lobby of a Honolulu hotel.

It was so wonderful that Frank's parents were able to come and see him. We enjoyed a nice few days together. I had never spent much time with them, so it was a good opportunity to spend a relaxed visit to get to know them better. When we got the very bad news that he would be returning to Vietnam, I took Frank over to Kona for a few days so he could meet my friends and see where I lived and worked. An acquaintance with a big tourist catamaran took us out on the ocean for snorkeling and dinner on the beach, free of charge. Then, a third difficult farewell.

REFLECTION ON CHAPTER TWENTY SIX
GOING HOME

Norfolk, Virginia

Frank had to do overnight duty on the ship quite a bit, so there were many quiet nights - just our cat Mickey, me, and that old black and white TV. I got to know Johnny Carson well. Alone on Christmas Eve, I watched Tiny Tim (Tiptoe Through the Tulips, cue the ukulele!) wed Miss Vicki on the Tonight Show. Frank came home Christmas morning, and we were shocked when our doorbell rang and the Postman delivered a Santa box from my mom with homemade stockings full of goodies! It was our first Christmas together, and we celebrated our second wedding anniversary the next day.

Thank heaven for Karen Winch. At social functions, the Navy officers' wives were polite to us, but we Marine wives were not part of the "family" and had to stick together. The Navy was a whole new culture, as well as different insignias! I had to buy some new clothes and a coat for the holiday parties, since our nicest clothes were hanging in the back seat of the car when everything had been stolen in Kansas City. Surely the sun must have come out at some point in those three months, but I don't remember it. On our way back west in March, we explored curvy hilly roads and new territory in West Virginia and Kentucky with the motorcycle hanging off Trigger's back bumper. Back to Colorado for a few days, we then drove from blizzard to sunny blooming Arizona the first of April, 1970.

Marine Corps Air Station, Yuma, Arizona

Not long after we moved to Yuma, temporarily living in the apartment in town, there was a costume party at the Officers' Club on base. I had made friends with my artistic neighbor,

Frank, Mickey, and the BSA on Trigger, in route to Yuma, AZ

Diana and Mickey taking the leap while leaving VA for AZ

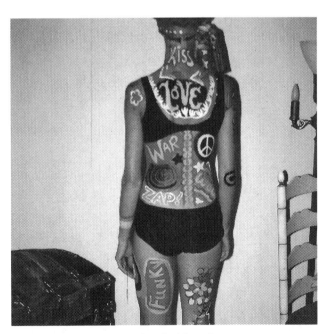

Diana's "Far Out" costume

Jeannie. For my costume, I put on a black two-piece bathing suit and the two of us spent the afternoon painting colorful psychedelic patterns all over my body with acrylic paint. I now cringe to think how others may have perceived the new athletic director and his wife - hey, it was 1970! (As John Denver would say, "Far out!")

During the summer that we lived in married officers' housing on the Marine Corps Air Station, a record was set for the number of consecutive days over 115 degrees. I learned to take a sweater to a restaurant or the movie theater in town, because it was always freezing with air conditioning over-kill. It was a great place to be pregnant in the winter where it was warm enough to ride my bike to the PX and Commissary and sit on our patio and read lots of books. In the spring the pool opened and I hung out with many other pregnant Marine wives in our maternity swimsuits. (Many girls named "Jennifer" born that year.) I did have to give up those fun desert trips on our motorcycle at some point, so Frank went out by himself to "plink around" with his pistol and brought back a few hefty lifeless rattlesnakes. Probably the most relaxed, laid-back time of my life, ever. The calm before the storm.

Following the athletic teams was enjoyable and a good way to see more of Arizona. I clearly remember the drive across the AZ desert in the non-air-conditioned gray Navy pickup truck in the middle of that summer. Frank wasn't supposed to be out of uniform, but no way was I going to mess up that crisply pressed shirt with water spray. The pavement was so hot it was amazing that it wasn't squishy. A non air-conditioned truck in Yuma, Arizona? Perhaps some Navy supply officer confused shipping orders with Alaska.

At this point we had very little furniture, so we bought a new blue crushed velvet hide-a-bed sofa and a queen sized bed, and filled in with some garage sale chairs and table that we refinished. There was a nice wood shop on base so Frank made us a stereo cabinet/book shelf and a locked gun cabinet that are still in use.

We had many friends in officer's housing, but still cherish our friendship with then-neighbors Bob and Vicki Russell to this day. We enjoyed many parties, dinners and picnics, bridge games, and a California camping trip with them. One crazy evening we were "helping" the athletic director chase rabbits off his football field by driving our motorcycles all over it. We have lived near them twice again in our nomadic lives, and Vicki has been a reader for this book.

I apologize to the adorable MCAS Yuma Marines at the gate who saluted (the officer's sticker on the front bumper of our faithful Dodge Charger) every time I drove in to the base without Frank - because I often smiled and flashed a peace sign. Perhaps they interpreted it as "victory".... .

Sports Parade

J. Carl Guymon

As March rushes to a close, and April slips up on us, we think it most appropriate to take time out, toss a fresh towel and give a journalistic pat on the fanny to the departing station athletic officer, Capt. Frank A. Hill.

Like the weary basketball player, who having led his team to a big lead late in the game, Capt. Hill deserves a breather. As of 1 April he'll be sitting on a civilian bench, though, as his active duty in the "green machine" is terminated.

Since beginning the difficult job as athletic officer, approximately a year ago, Capt. Hill has tirelessly worked to improve it. During his tenure, the gymnasium's locker room has had added to it a sauna bath. We now have a little guys basketball league, little league baseball and an MCAS officials association, which has greatly improved the quality and efficiency of the station's intramural officiating procedures.

All these aspects of the intramural and athletic program, not counting the regular sports, have been improved or implemented by Capt. Hill's perseverance and enthusiasm. The job, like many others, is a thankless position. Nothing is said until something goes wrong.

Capt. R. M. Stein, special services officer, is especially sympathetic to the problems of the athletic officer and knows that Hill will be sorely missed.

"He's done an outstanding job," Capt. Stein said. "He's made the athletic department a smooth running operation with a minimum amount of men, and he's had a large turnover of men, yet been able to snap them in and keep things running."

Capt. Stein pointed out that Hill has worked hard in sending MCAS athletes to various Arizona Interservice League and All-Marine events and has kept abreast of the sports situation in the city of Yuma, coordinating the station's programs to avoid conflicts.

"It's going to be hard to replace him," Capt. Stein said more than a bit wistfully, since he has drawn the lot to temporarily mind the athletic store until a replacement is found.

So, hats off to Capt. Hill for a job **well** done.

217

ABOUT THE LETTERS
UNREAD FOR 42 YEARS

Initially Frank just wanted to jot down his memoir in a casual way for family and close friends. I knew that he was a good "round the campfire" storyteller, so I dragged him to Trish Warner McCall's new writing class at our church. This book is the result of her coaching and much encouragement from others. It was Trish's idea to include the actual letters, and for me to add my side of the story.

Frank's 176 letters were neatly saved in a shoebox in 1969, then stored in a trunk with other Marine Corps memorabilia. He had not read them. The trunk stayed in my parents' basement in Littleton until we moved back to Colorado in 1977. Every few years, we would comment, "We should get out those letters," but it never happened until late 2011 when Frank was retired and ready to write his memoir. The photographs were taken on an Instamatic camera. Frank and I mailed film cartridges back and forth, and I had the photos developed immediately. They were put into an album that we did look at over the years.

Why didn't we open that shoebox for forty two years? Perhaps the idea just seemed too painful. It looked like an overwhelming task. We were too busy working and raising kids. "We'll get to it one of these days." Personally, I was afraid it would bring back symptoms of PTSD, and in subtle ways it did, as he immersed himself in the past while reading the letters. "To everything, there is a season." We didn't open them because it wasn't the right time, until now.

Diana

TYPED LETTERS

The monsoons are here and it will be pretty wet for the next 6 mo. We got some shots today, one was in the butt and it sure did hurt. Malaria pills and what not. This is a cool base, wish my tour was here. We had a secret briefing today and it scared the poop right out of me. I went to cash sales and picked up a few socks, skivvies, one set utilities and found some old boots someone threw away. They will at least get me to Nam and save $8.00.

They have mama sans here that come in, clean your room, wash clothes and shine shoes for 75 cents. A taxi anywhere is 25 cents. Drinks in the officer's bar are 30 cents. I wonder what happy hour is like. Well, I need to get a haircut (35 cents) and it is next to the post offices plus I'm going to the gift shop. Now, if they will mail it you can expect something, but if they don't , I can't take time to, we have to leave for the plane by 2000 hr. I'll be getting my platoon, tomorrow I guess. It is like a football game. I'm scared to death but hope to settle down when the action starts. I know you are sleeping now or you should be, pleasant dreams. I miss you very much because there was one hell of an emptiness when you got on that plane. I wish I would have kissed you more.

Your loving husband all ways,

Frank

Diana!

We are still in Division Rear trying to get to An Hoa where the 5th Regiment is located. Just sitting here for 3 days gives me little to write about; so I'm going to give you a mental picture of Division rear. The buildings are all on stilts about 1 or 2 ft. high constructed of plywood and tin roofs, screens are on most of the walls. We have one cot and blanket to sleep on and this is more than most of the troops have. They sleep in their poncho on the floor. No hot water and there are water hours. Trucks are running all over the place, we are near the 11th Motor Transport area. The urinal is a 55 gal. drum in the ground and the crapper is just an out door head. The perimeter is about ½ mile on top of this hill and last nite I was going to the head and noticed a few tracers zipping off the hill and a few hand grenades going off.

OCTOBER 21, 1968 | AN HOA | PAGE 11

Dear Diana,

It is 7:10 where you are and I'm finally in An Hoa with mud ankle deep. We finally got on a helo and in 15 min. here we are. Boy! This has to be a first writing you too letters in the same day within 8 hours. But enjoy it while you can you may not get but one a week or less while I'm in the field. So don't worry if you don't get a letter right off the bat! Ok? Every day that is. There was nothing but water between Da Nang & An Hoa! Now I can see why it is so difficult to get in here. I wish they would give me a weapon. I would feel a little better. We have been didy-bopping around where anybody could come in and hit us. I think I'll write more when I get to my battalion.

The platoon commander that preceded me was killed by an ambush, Aug 29th. So now my rattle is really shaken up. Delta 1/5 is the best in the Bn. They have killed the most NVA & VC and like wise taken more casualties. I'm worried but it must be worth it or I would not be here. Would I? Arty (Artillery) is really pounding away tonight. I wonder if I'll get any sleep tonite. Don't forget my absent –T ballot although I believe it is too late now! The time is now or never. Let it be now! OH God, I pray I want to see you again!

Good night
Love Frank

OCTOBER 23, 1968 | AN HOA | PAGE 13

Diana,

It is 10:00 A.M. Oct. 23 in Colo. now. I'll bet there is a frost in the air and the back range is pure white. This country could be beautiful if there was no war going on. I'm going to the bush on Sat. the 26th. I don't know if you got that paper I sent or not, but I'm taking over the 1st Plt. The one that was over ran with hand to hand combat. But don't worry that very rarely happens. A phantom jet made an air strike just out side of the perimeter this morning. It looks like a little bug then bright lights jet out from under its wings (rockets) and it pulls up and through the clouds. Now they are firing those illumination rounds into the "Arizona" area north of us. (Refer to paper "Sea Tiger") I'll be joining the Co. when they are in that region. If this type of stuff bugs you let me know & I won't write it.

NOVEMBER 10, 1968 | IN THE BUSH | PAGE 20

Dearest Diana

Left for the field 3 days ago. I've had 2 men wounded by friendly fire. I'll try to tell as much as I can so it will be messy. My platoon is by ourselves working with another company up in the "Horseshoe". I set up a tight perimeter the night of the 7th in a small vill about 25 by 50 meters. The tree line came right up to our perimeter. About 05:00 the next morning we got a few hand grenades from VC thrown our way. They landed just at the edge of our perim. Scared the shit right out of me. I don't think I've slept 2 hr. since. Earlier that day my point man came up on a VC running across a sandy area into the tall grass. I called in 18 81mm mortar rounds but did not get him. He was out of small arms range. So far I haven't had a rifle round in my direction, but a hand grenade is bad enough.

North into the "horseshoe" to link up with Charlie Company. They have the NVA backed up against the river and they need my Plt.

To fill a gap in the lines. Ever since we have been here we have been getting screwed. We have gotten only 1 meal a day and doing most of the work. We have a larger perimeter than the other platoons and they have no discipline. Last night my machine gun team captured two men of military age hiding out. I believe them to be VC or NVA. However the company commander is disagreeing with me. He is a Capt. & me a Lt. what the hell can I do. Well, I'll tell you this is not like basic school. I'm bitch'n and he doesn't like it a bit. I'm here to look out for my men and I don't call putting 32 men over a 900 meter line looking after them.

NOVEMBER 19, 1968 | IN THE BUSH | PAGE 29

Dearest Diana

We have been moving all over. Mostly collecting rice and flying it out! Yesterday my platoon found 3500 lbs. of rice in 3 houches (homes). We sacked it and called in a helo. As the chopper was lifting it out we started to take sniper fire. We returned fire and the chopper made it out. Then we got the hell out of there and bombed the shit out of them. We changed our position and last night one of our patrols was hit by gooks. No casualties but on the way in this morning they tripped a booby trap and one person received minor wounds… "lucky". But here is the kicker. Today I made my first kill and almost got it in the process. I took my Plt. out this morning on a patrol. As we entered this vill to check for ID's and VC suspects this mama san came around the corner of a houch leading a water buffalo and a calf. Man! That was all she wrote. The buffalo started to charge me. I kicked my M-16 off safety and retreated doing a nifty back step while at the same time pumping rounds into the huge beast baring down on me. Then I stumbled and Brayton (a trooper on my right) opened. The force of his bullets striking the buffalo knocked it off balance and it missed me by a few feet. He finally dropped dead about 10 ft. away. Needless to say I was shook up. That is the closest call I've had here yet. But I'm sure there will be closer and not with water buffaloes.

NOVEMBER 30, 1968 | IN THE BUSH | PAGE 40

Dearest Diana

We had hot turkey yesterday and everyone's moral is much better. We are, and have been, on road security between An Hoa and Liberty Bridge since the 23rd so we may be going into the bridge soon and have a little bit of slack time for 5 or 6 days.

We have been here so long I've made pretty good friends with this old papa san in the vill at the bottom of the hill. When we make water runs he is right their with a wash basin and boo-coo (Vietnamese for very much) water. Then he would sharpen my knife razor sharp and tell me with sign language how he had many relatives in this vill and in An Hoa and how he caught fish in basket traps and show me food like snails and all that. He probably has a dozen rifles and hand grenades stashed somewhere also. Oh well, friends by day enemy by nite. What a shitty war. Well, now I'm going to go down to papa san and shave and clean up. I'll take a camera and get a few shots.

JANUARY 22, 1969 | IN THE BUSH | PAGE 48

Dearest Diana,

Last night we made a night move from the Horseshoe to a vill we use to occupy. As we entered the area we were fired upon and we saw the gooks "sky-out". So we opened up and killed two. Later the same thing happened but a mama-san got in the way and she got it. The march took 14 hrs. and we only came 4 mi, and I give you one guess who was point. Yup, me! [Meaning my platoon was point, not me personally.]

DECEMBER 3, 1968 | IN THE BUSH | PAGE 54

On my patrol yesterday we got opened up on and luckily no one was hurt. We were walking across a patty dike and all of a sudden we took automatic weapons fire from the front. I was 5th man back. I never hit the deck so fast in my life. Right off the dike into the mud and slime, but it felt good. We returned fire and shot some arty at them. This happened two or three times more and then we headed back home. When we started taking fire from a vill we shot artillery in it and then fired small arms. Upon entering the only person dead was a 4 yr. old girl. They get rid of the dead enemy so fast. Primarily because of the psychological effect. If you never see what you are killing you get quite frustrated.

JANUARY 25, 1969 | IN THE BUSH | PAGE 63

Dearest Diana

We got up early this morning and hit a village. As we went toward the vill my point man saw a gook and killed him. He had some NVA uniforms, and AK-47 assault rifle, chicom hand grenades and magazines for the rifle. We completely checked the vill and found nothing much. Then I put my radio on a frequency which is used by observation planes and had an aerial observer circle me all the way back to base camp. Sometimes the field isn't so bad. There is just one thing wrong with this place! You can get killed. Otherwise you make mucho $, get a good tan & OH, I forgot, one other thin that sucks about VN, being away from you. I guess that is the worst of all.

DECEMBER 18, 1968 | IN THE BUSH | PAGE 71-76

Dearest Diana,

Last night will be a night I'm sure I will relive in a thousand dreams. I gunned down a man & woman. They were undoubtedly VC. Last night my Plt. and I received an order to set up a night ambush in the region called the Horseshoe; about a mile and ½ from the base camp. The 7th Marines were on a big push, so they thought we would get some as they tried to make their escape at night. I knew the region quite well having operated in it my first few days in the bush. We waited until dark and moved out. The going wasn't bad at all. We moved with extreme care and quietness. By 8:30 we had reached our area to set up. It faced north on a 10 ft. high sand bar overlooking a wide stretch of sand. Behind us stood tall elephant grass with a small village about 200 meters to our rear. As we set in we heard voices and activity from the village. All went well until 05:45 when I was on watch. I happened to look to my left and saw 3 figures walking onto the sand bar about 75 meters away. I immediately got over to the machine gun position and alerted them. My M-16 was full of tracer ammo so the kill zone could be marked by my burst of automatic fire. As they walked closer I moved to the front of my lines and tried to snap off my safety. It would not budge. Then it clicked off with a noise sent chills down my spine. The 3 figures stopped and crouched for a split second it seemed like eternity. Then I opened up. The light of the tracers made it possible to see the bullets striking the people... they were so close. Then my machine guns opened up and all was still. Two bodies lay before us. One got away but let a trail of blood.

We stayed in our position until the dawn made it possible to go out and pull in the bodies. Two VC. One a man with over $150.00 in South Vietnamese money and a safe conduct pass through VC country. The woman had bandages & Rice. They must have been aiding the VC. No weapons were on the bodies so I'll always wonder. But all the Vietnamese know you don't move after dark or before first light. They were helping the enemy, plus no civilian runs around with that kind of money. After it was all over I started to shake like a leaf. What if they would have had weapons when my safety wouldn't go off? Things like that scared the hell out of me. But it is all over now. Now I know what it is like to kill a person... even unarmed in this war. I have no compassion. I'm not proud of it but neither am I resentful of it. I'll get over it. Most ricky-tick. Well, how have you been? Don't sent any more vitamins unless I ask for them. I'm sending a small pair of binoculars I borrowed in the field and messed up so bought them from the man & just as soon send them home as have to hump them in the field.

We are going out to the bush as a company tomorrow. Lt. Jones was sent to the rear. He messed up and they don't want him in the field. Now I've got the most bush time of any of the Lieutenants. In the company!!! Our new company commander is a 1st Lieutenant if you didn't know.

This is really a screwed up letter. I don't know how you will be able to read it. Maybe in another 2 or 3 months they will jerk me out of the bush as they did Lt. Jones. They say I'm doing a good job, well I hope that does not mean more bush time. Get the bad ones out put the good ones in. If that is the case maybe I should do a bad job. But you know that is not the case. It's possible something like that would cost a man's life & then I would have something on my conscience. There is less & less to talk about. I hate to put so much of that junk like the first of this letter. But that is what I'm doing. Unfortunately I don't think anything could make a person more homesick than war! Over 40 day's now... all I have to do is last 80 more and it will be close.

How do you write a letter to someone you miss so much, love so much and want see again so much. It is most difficult believe me. I wish you could be in a little bullet proof box and ride around on my pack so you could see what I'm doing. It is so strange to have 50 men's lives in the balance of my decisions. They come to me for advice on this & that and it seems short a time since I was in their shoes. The men are great, but their job sucks. They have 13 mo. of this while officers have 6-7. The troops get the short end every time. And you, you are getting the short end. But wait till Hawaii we will see you get the long end then...Ok?

You are the only one,
Love Hug

DECEMBER 24, 1968 | IN THE BUSH | PAGE 83

Dearest Diana

I hope this letter gets to you before the man in "blue". Yes! I've been wounded. Most lucky to still be around. The wound is not serious at all. A piece of shrapnel went through the back of my flak jacket and just cut the flesh. Nothing to worry about. They just put a band-aid on it and that was all. I won't even be taken out of the field, so you know it is not serious.

We were on patrol this morning when I must have tripped a boo-by-trap. All of a sudden it exploded between me and my radio man. He got the worst of it. Shrapnel all over his body. I was about 10 ft. away and the blast just stunned me and knocked me off my feet. At the same time I felt this hot burning in the middle of my back. A small piece about the size of a match head went through the flak. If I hadn't had it on it would have put a hole through me most likely. Two more and I go out of this country. I'll settle for no more and make it home in a few extra months.

Well here it is Xmas Eve and it sure doesn't seem like it here. But how could it out here? The truce starts at 1800 today & ends at 1800 tomorrow on the 25th. I think tonight they will break it. It seems strange but having grenades go off 10 & 15 yards away is getting to be common place. Every time my Plt does something it gets hit or hits something. Never will I be so thankful as today. It is too bad my radio man was hurt so badly. He had shrapnel all through his body, both legs & arms and neck. There must be something I can talk about other than this ~~fucking~~ war.

JANUARY 13, 1969 | BATTALION HEADQUARTERS, LIBERTY BRIDGE | PAGE 91

Dearest Diana,

Well, here we are over the 3 mo. mark starting #4. A lot has happened or I should say I have got some news since the tape. As for the tape you can send one back if you want but don't buy a recorder because there is plenty in my Plt. They're not going to get me babe; they can't do it, I'm too mean.

More news! Would you believe that I have more bush time than all the other Plt. Commanders in the Bn! (Battalion) That means if no one gets bumped off I'll be the next pulled out of the bush. S-4 school? That means about one more month in the bush, and right in the middle of the worst time, TET! But like I said we're going to make it. We are all rested up and ready to go. We will be moving into the "Horseshoe". They have been bombing the hell out of it and the New Jersey has been shelling the area also. We will be moving into the "shoe" on the 16th it will last a few days and then we will probably move south and operate. Guess who is point for that night move into the shoe? Yup, my platoon. Well I guess we should be. After all I have the best Plt. I have been steadily improving my short timers stick. Now I've put on a 50 caliber point on it. It helps quite a bit at night. Keeps me from running into obstacles or falling into holes. Boy!

JANUARY 20, 1969 | IN THE BUSH | PAGE 93

Dearest Diana

We have been on an operation now for five days. That is one of the reasons I have not had the time to write. Today we have a little slack time while the ARVN's push toward us. Bad news! Our captain was injured pretty badly yesterday, stepped on a booby trap. He got shrapnel all over his body and in his elbow. He won't be back! Most likely he will be in the rear or sent back to the states. I've been a little sick the last few nights. I have the runs and puked a few times last night. I'm feeling somewhat better today though and I'm losing wt. The heat is a bitch. I'm sure getting sick of this shit. An the worst is yet to come! "TET" The first few days of this operation we captured a communications officer and many maps and intelligence for TET. My platoon did the greater part of it. We killed about 6 gooks that day also. Well!

I heard today that one or two lieutenants that were ahead of me have now left the bush. I sure wish they would get to me. One way or the other I'm not going to return to the bush after R&R. So don't worry. I will have already had mucho time in. I should not kick though! The grunts have to put in 13 mo in the bush. I can't see that. Maybe they can understand the pressure. Sometimes I think I'm going off my rocker. I hate to send this letter since it is so depressing because I sure am down in the dumps. Well, maybe things will look up in March. I think you are right. Those packages probably went down with that plane. So send a few more oysters, artichoke hearts..etc. If you don't mind I guess I'm going to need a few more watch band pins after all. The other day one of my men was burned and as I threw off my flack gear ripped off my watch. So send a few more. What is this about you gaining wt? How much do you weight? You aren't sick are you? Take care of yourself for Christ's sake. After all, you are all I have. Or I should say all I ever want! Oh, Hum! Absence makes the heart grow fonder. See what you do for me just sitting here talking to you makes me feel better. I love you.

FEBRUARY 3, 1969 | IN THE BUSH | PAGE 108

Today was my worst in Vietnam to date. One of my best men died today. We were making a night march and I was point as usual. We entered this vill and gooks took off running. We opened up killing 3 and captured 3. We decided to search out the area and found rockets and medical supplies. We continued to search and a man from 3rd Plt. hit a white phosphorous booby trap resulting in very serious burns on his legs. We decided there must be something important if they booby trapped that tree line so about five of us decided to go in and check it out. Then something else occupied my attention and the others went on in. All of a sudden there was this massive explosion. I knew immediately what it was and knew they were all killed. Skip Bye, the boy I lost, stepped on a 155mm cannon shell. I couldn't look at the body. I just heard what it looked like and I'll leave it at that. He was an outstanding Marine and did a fantastic job in place of Sgt. Powell. I thank God I wasn't with him. I'm so sorry for his wife. He just had a baby girl two weeks ago and for the first time in a long time I wept like a baby. I'm really scared Diana. I've had so many close calls. I sure hope I don't have to go back to the bush after R&R. I know I won't feel like it. I feel so strange right now. I'm alive. I can see, feel, breath, and taste, for what? Why? What is Life? Something that should be valued so much? He felt no pain! Yet just 5 minutes before he died we were laughing and joking around. Maybe that is why it hit me so hard at first. I guess I'm not as hard as the outside looks. Today I'm sad. I can't write a happy letter so I'll close. I'm sorry if you are sad now. I'll do my best to make you happy in Hawaii. Diana, thanks for the pics they are number one. I love you so much.

Your loving husband for ever & ever,
Frank

FEBRUARY 11, 1969 | LIBERTY BRIDGE | PAGE 132

Dear Diana,

I'm not sure about what is going on, but today a new 2nd Lt. came into our company and he is taking over my platoon! Sounds like it's out of the bush for me! Eh? His name is Pilkington and he graduated from basic school in November and went to HILT (Hilton Head), that is why he is just getting over here. But that is OK with me just as long as he is here. Tomorrow we are going to run a patrol together and then he will most likely take it over lock-stock & barrel. Yahooooo! And in 17 days I'll be seeing you in Hawaii for a hell of a good time. OK?

About 3 hrs. later and I'm just nervous as all get out because I don't know what they have in store for me. Wish they would be more concrete as to what I'm going to be doing. Time will go so much slowly now, since I haven't got a platoon of my own. I guess I'll just join the C.P. and remain there until I leave for R&R.

MARCH 10, 1969 | IN THE BUSH | PAGE 134

Dearest Diana,

I just finished a patrol this morning down past Phu Loc (2). Right now we are on a hill just off a road near My Lac (2) about 913513. Boy! Have I got a bad attitude now that I'm back in the bush. And I'm twice as worried as ever! I'm sure it is because of the outstanding time we had on R&R. I didn't believe I was in such bad shape until that patrol today when I was walking along and sweating like crazy. Plus my trousers don't fit either. Boy! Did I get spoiled? But it was fun. I can't believe it was over so fast. Will I ever be glad to get back to the rear where I can at least feel clean once in a while. I can't find anything to say. I'm in such as shitty mood. I shouldn't even be writing a letter because it probably depresses you also. No sooner had I gotten back to the bush and I could roll the dirt off me.

Now I am the third platoon Commander. They are not as good as the "Fighting First" but better than some I have seen. The big thing is I don't know how long I'm going to be here. Surely not more than a month I hope!?!?! Things are drying up and it is getting hotter. I'm cooking, I can't even imagine what summer will be like. Why is it I miss you so much just after having been with you not more than a week ago? But I feel worse than when I first left. Wish I would get a letter from you. Should be pretty soon. If you wrote the day I left, but I'm sure you were too busy. How is Kona? Nice and out of the way? Wish I was there but may as well wish for the moon! I'm is a cruddy mood so I'll close for now. Maybe I feel better tomorrow. Thanks for such a wonderful time in Hawaii. I'll never forget it as long as we live. Be a good kid and put on some pounds (in the right places). I love you so much it hurts.

Frank

MARCH 15, 1969 | LIBERTY BRIDGE | PAGE 136

Dearest Diana,

I'm on the other side of the bridge and this is the side where people hang a little bit more loosely and do a little too much drinking. I haven't touched a drop since R&R! Just finished "The President's Plane Is Missing". Not too bad! I'm surprised it held my interest. Received your letter of the 8th. Your new job sounds nice. Meet quite a few people. You said the people are so nice and casual. Just make sure you don't get toooo casual with the natives! The "deli" sounds great! I haven't lost any wt. yet. I have actually only been in the bush for 3 days and it has been quiet like I have never seen. I think all their man power is centered around the bigger installations during the offensive. I've given up my frustration about not knowing my immediate destiny. And resigned to the fact that I'm in the bush and I'll stay here until (?). I just psyched myself out to the fact. Your letters sound so cheery. I'm sure happy you seem so much more at ease or something now. Like the flower budding or something reincarnating. There is a world of difference in your letters. You can't tell, but I sure can. I think you will enjoy your job, etc. & put on some wt. But not too much, OK. Not over 130 lb. OK? One thing I regret about your job is you won't be able to write so often on the job as you did at the bank, but maybe the goodies will suffice.

MARCH 19, 1969 | LIBERTY BRIDGE | PAGE 143

Dearest Wife,

One year ago today I graduated [from CSU] and was commissioned! Time sure has gone by fast! I just hope it continues to pass by as fast. Last night we took 5 or 6 incoming rockets that just missed the ammo dump. The other side of the bridge had a full fledged attack. They got inside the wire and started blowing bunkers and buildings. Fifteen were killed and 70 some gooks got it. I'm sure you will hear about it if you haven't already.

Anyway they sure paid for it. They must have been doped up on drugs because it was sure a suicide mission. Some were found with hands and legs blown off and still fighting with tourniquets on their stumps. It was a real blood bath. I'm glad I wasn't on that side of the bridge. I don't know when we will be going back to the bush. Soon I hope. This stuff is getting old.

MARCH 22, 1969 | AN HOA | PAGE 146

Dear Diana,

Remember the trouble I was having with my guts on R&R? Well, it seemed to be getting worse instead of better so I came in to An Hoa the 20th to have it looked into. They took a sample of my "stool" (shit) and said they found nothing. But the doc asked how long I have had the runs. So when I said over a month he sent me to 1st Medical Battalion in Da Nang. There they took another stool sample, blood sample and stuck tubes and pipes up my ass!!! And it hurt. Well, they decided I have Hookworm (from going barefoot), and vasilary dysentery. In other words the chronic shits with bugs. They gave me 3 different types of medications (oral) to take in sequence. One of the pills is suppose to give me a real buzz. So I'm not supposed to be in the bush when I take it. That means I'll probably go to the bridge the 26th or 27th.

Did you hear about the bridge? We were attacked the 18th I believe and 72 gooks were killed on the wire or inside the wire surrounding the compound. I may have already mentioned something about it. I can't remember so I'll keep going. They had flame throwers and satchel charges with an unbelievable amount of hand grenades. Unfortunately 4 people from our unit died and 8 people from the artillery battery. Over 50 people were medevacuated out the next day and they had to dig a hole with a bulldozer to bury all the dead gooks. The VC & NVA paid a high price for what they accomplished. It is amazing that so many got inside the barbed wire surrounding the Place! Right now I'm in An Hoa and we have a new Captain to take over.

Dear Diana,

I received your letter of the 30th today. Went to the movies last night with Stuart. Cool! I'm jealous. How do you expect me to feel while you are dating some guy I don't know a thing about and I sit here helpless. You must look pretty good at 125 lbs. You always did. In your letters you always say we did this, meet the gang, the group, or the crowd. I'm sure you are always next to Stuart, or him next to you. I thought his old girl friend was suppose to go with him around the world. How come all of a sudden he stays in Kona? And around you? You are married and he doesn't or should know better than to hang around another man's wife! I'll be coming to Kona sometime between now and July 31. You won't know when, and I'm not going to say. I think I'll just pop in and when I do tell Stuart to stand by. Because if he is with you and I don't care where or what we are going to tangle. And don't try to tell me his intentions are good. I don't believe it. I never will. He is male your are female, figure it out! I can tell by your letters your love for me is waning. And you don't miss me anymore because you have someone else to fill the gap. Now don't get me wrong, Diana. I don't think you are being unfaithful, but how long will your will power hold out? I'll bet right now it is in the "Big Brother" stage where you talk very seriously about your problems and worries. Most of which I'm sure concerns me. And he agrees, especially with your love for me and says how lucky a person I am to have a wife like you. I thought those girls would provide you with enough companionship. A kid just walked in with a letter for me from Mom. Says she is sick…Oh Hell, I'll just send it to you. Now back to you and Stuart. I'm so damn jealous I have a sick feeling in my stomach, and feel weak all over. I didn't know I could even love you this much. But it is so strong and tell you how I feel. Nothing to release it on. Maybe if I go back to the bush it will take my mind off of it. Plus maybe I'll have something to vent my frustration on. I have no weapon against Stuart except the love you have or had for me. I have to rely on this and your good judgment. I had so much faith in you but it seems to be shaken a little. Most of all be truthful in telling me what you are doing in your spare time. I want to know. But most of all I want you for the rest of my life. And as I said before I won't share any part of you anytime, anywhere. It's all or none Diana.

Guess what! The kid just came in with a package from you. It has a green chickie so I'll wear it in my rubber band around my helmet for as long as it will stay in one piece or until some general tells me to take it off. And the Easter basket is in A-1 shape. Thank you. You had 3 Black Russians! With who? And on our anniversary. How would you feel if I went out and had three drinks with some girl, after I had taken her to a movie? Don't go out with him anymore, Diana. I don't like it. And you don't need it. You haven't got problems so bad you need a big brother. I don't trust him. I've got to catch a helicopter out to Charlie Co. to pay them. They're in the Horseshoe.

Love, Frank

MAY 16, 1969 | LIBERTY BRIDGE | PAGE 156

Dearest Diana,

Right now I'm at the bridge and have spent the last two nights and days here. Well, Babe, things don't look so good for the kid! I believe they are going to make me Company Commander of H&S Co. and we will be going to the Arizona "bush". While we are discussing bad news, remember Lt. Pilkington, the Lt. that took over my Plt? He was killed two days ago, not over 1000 yards. From the bridge. That was a real bust! He was a damn fine Lt. and he was married to a very good looking woman. Fortunately, they had no children. What is the thing that makes the difference whether it is me or Pilkington? He was a good friend and I feel a great loss now. Anytime someone I know dies I feel a loss, but this seems like such a waste. I'd better stop philosophizing or I'll really get down in the dumps.

MAY 23, 1969 | GUAM NAVAL HOSPITAL | PAGE 168-171

Dear Diana,

It is 11:00 the 23rd (May) and this is the first time I have had a chance to write with all the needles and stuff taken out. Well I'll give you the straight scoop. I got a hole in my right thigh big enough to put your fist in. It is hard to write in this position. It was a 122 rocket that hit about 15 yrds away. A chunk of shrapnel about the size of a golf ball hit me dead center in the leg. Fortunately it came from my left front as I was facing the explosion and so it missed the bone. But the muscle & tissue damage is pretty extensive.

One doctor said it would be two months before I'm back to normal. I should be limping around in about 10 days. They are letting it drain now and going to sew it up Monday. The inside of my leg looks like a beef steak.

Some of the other patients think I may be sent home. I don't know for sure but I believe it is possible. At any rate I'm not getting my hopes up for anything. If they do send me back, I'm going to beg for a job at Division. And if they do maybe you can fly down and spend the last few weeks in Guam with me. Then I'll ask for R&R in September. We'll fix'em. Of course it would be much better if they just shipped me home!

Everything else is fine I may lose some weight or get a little puffy being laid up for so long but I'll get back in shape. So the best thing to do is stay put, keep right on doing what you have been and wait until they decide what they are going to do with me. One way or the other we'll see each other in Aug. or sooner. I'm kinda pooped so I'm going to sleep a bit. Now I miss you more than ever. I never knew how much you meant until that metal hit me. God, I pray they don't send me back.

I love you, Frank

AUGUST 24, 1969 | DA NANG | PAGE 188

Dearest Diana,

It has been a long day. It started at 05:00 when Capt. Milici came storming into my hootch. The lines were getting hit in Charlie Sector and the Reaction Company was being called out. Well, we got saddled up and moved out. Our mission was to seal off the avenue of escape by trucking around the mountain to the blocking position. I went with the first platoon and set in a block facing the ridge line that had been attacked while another company swept down the slope. F-4 Phantoms were called in and one of our men was hit by a bomb fragment just below the knee. It broke both bones and stuck in, half out and half in like the blade of a hatchet. When the corpsman got to him the metal was still so hot it was sizzling in his flesh. They poured cold water on him and medevac'd him out. He will keep his leg but it will be a long time before he walks. When we returned we learned a lieutenant was killed during the early morning fighting. He was killed not far from the same place where I slept in the road. I wonder if there is an angel on my shoulder! Anyway, we waited in our blocking positions for over 4 hr. roasting the heat then came on in. Tonite I'm still on reactionary but hoping nothing will happen.

I haven't even had time to learn the General's brief for tomorrow. It will probably be a real lulu! If I keep this busy, who needs to worry about time going fast. Everything is so damn quiet while I'm gone then all Hell breaks loose when I return; it really pisses me off. Why? I'm glad I get off this reactionary Sept. 20 for R&R. I hate this getting set up all the time. In a way it is worse than the bush, because when they call you they are going to put you in the hottest spot. I got out of the frying pan into the fire! I just have the comforts of home here that is all. Fear is inversely proportionate to time remaining in Vietnam! Understand? Time ↓ Fear ↑ and thought of you and home are directly proportional.

APPENDIX

Douglas County News Press Article, November 12th, 1991.
From author's presentation to Parker Breakfast Club.

Vietnam veteran says Gulf War helped to justify his sacrifice

By Richard Bangs
News-Press Editor

Desert Storm has been a catharsis to at least one Vietnam veteran.

Frank Hill, Parker resident and Vietnam War veteran, said that the Persian Gulf War has made him think his service in Vietnam meant something.

"I praise the men and women who fought that war and I fully supported them," Hill told the Parker Breakfast Club Monday.

"For the first time I began to feel like the sacrifice of Vietnam was worth it – that the sacrifice finally meant something.

"After the Vietnam War, (our leaders) said no more Vietnams. I didn't believe it."

Hill said that he still didn't believe it as the Gulf War started but does now because of the way the war was conducted – fighting all out to win.

Hill was a Marine lieutenant in Vietnam and a platoon commander. During his tour of action he saw 27 men killed or wounded and that once on an ambush he was the one who had to shoot two Vietnamese.

Hill said he was proud of his service in the war "but, I harbor deep resentment for the way the war was conducted and the way the country was run at home."

After returning from the war, Hill said, he had little trouble as-similating back into society and didn't experience the negativism that other veterans did.

He said he did, however, have some problems dealing with his war experience and became active in Point Man, a Christian-based ecumenical group for combat veterans.

"I credit my ability to function in today's society to Christian counseling," Hill said.

He said many Vietnam veterans are still experiencing Post Traumatic Stress Disorder. He said that often the shock of what happened to them in the war made their minds shut out experiences and refuse to deal with reality.

"It is a disconnecting, a disassociation with reality and that sometimes becomes a mechanism that can go on through life, in personal relations and at work."

He said PTSD can be triggered years later by something that reminds the person of his experiences, such as red dust, rain, a person or an event.

Hill said World War II veterans had PTSD but there was less media coverage of it so it was less visible.

Part of the reason for the distress, Hill said, is that the country has not grieved over the war.

"In getting over a traumatic event, you have to grieve. The U.S. has never grieved over Vietnam."

He said the last war the United States has grieved over was the Civil War because the "country has had no leaders to lead us through that process."

In answers to questions, Hill said he finds it difficult to believe there are still Americans being held in Vietnam against their will. "It would serve no purpose," he said.

He also said he would have no trouble normalizing relations with Vietnam and making trade agreements but would have trouble with giving aid to the country.

Hill said he thought television coverage of the Gulf War was good.

"It was good in that they didn't have correspondents in the field to watch us loading dead bodies in helicopters." They covered the facts without showing the carnage, he said.

He said Vietnam was a beautiful country with a peaceful agrarian society. He related one incident in which an old man in a village sharpened Hill's combat knife so sharp he could shave with it.

He later found the man had been killed by the Viet Cong, he said.

He said two good things had come from the Vietnam War. A strong bond has been formed with fellow soldiers with whom he keeps in touch with.

And, the country "has developed a strong resolve never to let it happen again. We will resist picking up arms, but if we have to, don't hold back."

TYPED EDITED ARTICLE ON FOLLOWING PAGE

Vietnam veteran says Gulf War helped to justify his sacrifice

Tuesday, Nov. 12, 1991 - Douglas County News Press
By Richard Bangs - *News-Press Editor*

Desert Storm has been a catharsis to at least one Vietnam veteran. Frank Hill, Parker resident and Vietnam War veteran, said that the Persian Gulf War has made him think his service in Vietnam meant something.

"I praise the men and women who fought that war and I fully supported them," Hill told the Parker Breakfast Club Monday. "For the first time I began to feel like the sacrifice of Vietnam was worth it - that the sacrifice finally meant something. After the Vietnam War, (our leaders) said no more Vietnams. I didn't believe it". Hill said that he still didn't believe it as the Gulf War started but does now because of the way the war was conducted - fighting all out to win.

Hill was a Marine lieutenant in Vietnam and a platoon commander. During his tour of action he saw 27 men killed or wounded and that once on an ambush he was the one who had to shoot two Vietnamese. He is proud of his service in the war "but, I harbor deep resentment for the way the war was conducted and the way the country was run at home."

After returning from the war, Hill said, he had little trouble assimilating back into society and didn't experience the negativism that other veterans did. However, he had some problems dealing with his war experience and became active in Point Man, A Christian-based ecumenical group for combat veterans. "I credit my ability to function in today's society to Christian counseling," Hill explained.

He said many Vietnam veterans are still experiencing Post Traumatic Stress Disorder and often the shock of what happened to them in the war made their minds shut out experiences and refuse to deal with reality. "It is a disconnecting, a disassociation with reality and that sometimes becomes a mechanism that can go on through life, in personal relations and work." According to Hill, PTSD can be triggered years later by something that reminds the person of his experiences, such as red dust, rain, a person or an event. He went on to share that World War II veterans had PTSD but there was less media coverage of it so it was less visible.

Part of the reason for the distress, Hill said, is that the country has not grieved over the war. "In getting over a traumatic event, you have to grieve. The U.S. has never grieved over Vietnam." Hill believes the last war the United States grieved over was the Civil War, because the "country has had no leaders to lead us through that process."

In answers to questions, Hill finds it difficult to believe there are still Americans being held in Vietnam against their will. "It would serve no purpose." He also confessed that he would have no trouble normalizing relations with Vietnam and making trade agreements but would have trouble with giving aid to the country.

Hill thought television coverage of the Gulf War was good. "It was good in that they didn't have correspondents in the field to watch us loading dead bodies in helicopters." They covered the facts without showing the carnage, he said.

He said Vietnam was a beautiful country with a peaceful agrarian society. He related one incident in which an old man in a village sharpened Hill's combat knife so sharp he could shave with it. He later found the man had been killed by the Viet Cong.

He said two good things had come from the Vietnam War. A strong bond has been formed with fellow soldiers with whom he keeps in touch with, and the country has developed a strong resolve to never let it happen again. We will resist picking up arms, but if we have to, don't hold back.

M61 FRAGMENTATION GRENADE

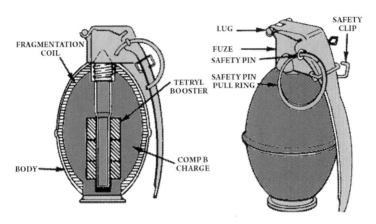

The lug, fuze and safety pin mechanism is one unit that can be unscrewed and removed to expose the explosive inside the grenade.

MILITARY RANKS
OF THE U.S. MARINE CORPS

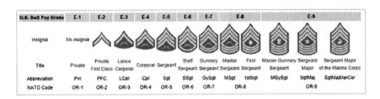

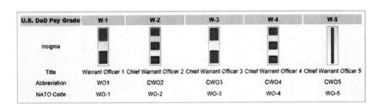

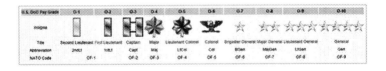